Table of Contents

A QUEENS DELIGHT OF Conserves, and Preserves, Candying and Distilling

To preserve white Pear Plums, or green.

To preserve Grapes

To preserve Quinces white.

To preserve Respass.

To preserve Pippins.

To preserve fruits green.

To preserve Oranges and Lemons the best way.

An approved Conserve for a Cough or Consumption of the Lungs.

To make conserve of Any of these Fruits.

To dry any Fruits after they are preserved, to or Candy them.

To preserve Artichokes young, green Walnuts and Lemons, and the

To preserve Quinces white or red.

To preserve Grapes.

To preserve Pippins, Apricoks, Pear-Plums and Peaches when they are

To preserve Pippins, Apricocks, Pear-Plums, or Peaches green.

To dry Pippins, or Pears without Sugar.

To make Syrup of Clove-gilly flowers.

To make Syrup of Hysop for Colds.

To make Orange Water.

To dry Cherries.

To make juyce of Liquorish.

A Perfume for Cloths, Gloves.

To make Almond Bisket.

To dry Apricocks.

To make Quinces for Pies.

The best way to break sweet Powder.

To make excellent Perfumes.

To make Conserve of Roses boiled.

To make Conserves of Roses unboiled.

To make a very good Pomatum.
To make Raisin Wine.
To make Rasberry Wine.
The best way to preserve Cherries.
A Tincture of Ambergreece.
To make Usquebath the best way.
To preserve Cherries with a quarter of their weights in Sugar.
To make Gelly of Pippins.
To make Apricock Cakes.
To preserve Barberries the best way.
To make Lozenges of Red Roses.
To make Chips of Quinces.
To make Sugar of Wormwood, Mint, Anniseed, or any other of that kinde.
To make Syrup of Lemons or Citrons.
To make Jambals of Apricocks or Quinces.
To make Cherry-water.
To make Orange Cakes.
To preserve Oranges the French way.
To preserve green Plums.
To dry Plums.
To preserve Cherries the best way, bigger than they grow naturally,
To preserve Damsins, red Plums or black.
To dry Pippins or Pears.
To dry Pippins or Pears another way.
To dry Apricocks tender.
To dry Plums.
To dry Apricocks.
Conserves of Violets the Italian manner.
Conserves of red Roses the Italian manner.
Conserve of Borage Flowers after the Italian manner.
Conserve of Rosemary flowers after the Italian manner.
Conserve of Betony after the Italian way.
Conserve of Sage.
Conserve of flowers of Lavender.
Conserve of Marjoram.
Conserve of Peony after the Italian way.
Touching Candies, as followeth.

To Candy Rosemary-flowers in the Sun.
To Make Sugar of Roses.
To Candy Pippins, Pears, Apricocks or Plums.
To Candy or clear Rockcandy flowers.
To Candy Spanish Flowers.
To Candy Grapes, Cherries or Barberries.
To Candy Suckets of Oranges, Lemons, Citrons, and Angelica.
To Candy the Orange Roots.
Candy Orange Peels after the Italian way.
To Candy Citrons after the Spanish way.
Candied Cherries, the Italian way.
Chicory Roots candied the Italian way.
Touching Marmalets, and Quiddony, as followeth.
To make Marmalet of Damsins.
To make white Marmalet of Quinces.
To make Marmalet of any tender Plum.
To make Orange Marmalet.
To make Quiddony of Pippins of Ruby or any Amber colour.
To make Quiddony of all kind of Plums.
To make Marmalet of Oranges, or Orange Cakes, &c.
Touching Pastrey and Pasties.
To_make_Sugar_Cakes.
To make clear Cakes of Plums.
To make Paste of Oranges and Lemons.
To make Rasberry Cakes.
To make Paste of Genoa Citrons.
To make a French Tart.
To make Cakes of Pear Plums.
To make Cakes, viz.
To make a Cake the way of the Royal Princess, the Lady Elizabeth,
To make Paste of Apricocks.
To make Paste of Pippins like leaves, and some like Plums, with their
To make Paste of Elecampane roots, an excellent remedy for the Cough of
To make Paste of flowers of the colour of Marble, tasting of natural
To make Paste of Rasberries or English Currans.
To make Naples Bisket.

To make Italian Biskets.

To make Prince Biskets

To make Marchpane to Ice and Gild, and garnish it according to Art.

Lozenges

To make Walnuts artificial.

To make Collops like Bacon of Marchpane.

To make artificial Fruits.

Touching Preserves and Pomanders.

To make an excellent perfume to burn between two Rose leaves.

To make Pomander.

To make an Ipswich Water.

To make a sweet Smell.

Touching Wine.

To make Hypocras.

The Lady Thornburghs *Syrup of Elders.*

To make gelly of Raspis the best way.

To dry Fox Skins.

Choice Secrets made known.

To make true Magistery of Pearl.

How to make Hair grow.

To write Letters of Secret, that they cannot be read without the

How to keep Wine from Sowring.

To take out Spots of Grease or Oyl.

To make hair grow black, though any colour.

King Edwards *perfume.*

Queen Elizabeths *Perfume.*

Mr. Ferene *of the* New Exchange, *Perfumer to the Queen, his rare*

To make the said Powder into Paste.

The Receipt of the Lady Kents *powder, presented by her Ladyship to*

A Cordial Water of Sir Walter Raleigh.

The Lady Malets Cordial Water.

A Sovereign Water of Dr. Stephens, *which he long times used,*

A Plague Water to be taken one spoonful every four hours with one sweat

Poppy water.

A Water for a Consumption, or for a Brain that is weak.

Another of the same.

A good Stomach Water.

A Bag of purging Ale.

The Ale of Health and Strength, by Viscount St. **Albans.**

A Water excellent good against the Plague.

A Cordial Cherry-water.

The Lord **Spencers** *Cherry-water.*

The Herbs to be distilled for Usquebath.

Dr. **Kings** *way to make Mead.*

To make Syrup of Rasberries.

To make Lemon Water.

To make Gilly-flower Wine.

The Lady **Spotswood** *Stomach Water.*

Water of Time for the Passion of the Heart.

A Receipt to make damnable Hum.

An admirable Water for sore Eyes.

A Snail Water for weak Children, and old People.

Clary Water for the Back, Stomach, &c.

Dr. **Montfords** *Cordial Water.*

Aqua Mirabilis, Sir **Kenelm Digby's** *way.*

A Water for fainting of the Heart.

A Surfeit Water.

Dr. **Butlers** *Cordial Water against Melancholly, &c. most approved.*

The admirable and most famous Snail Water.

A singular Mint water.

Distillings.

A most Excellent **Aqua Coelestis** *taught by Mr.* **Philips Apothecary.**

Hypocras taught by Dr. **Twine** *for Wind in the Stomach.*

Marigold flowers distilled, good for the pain of the Head.

A Water good for Sun burning.

The Lady **Giffords** *cordial Water.*

A water for one pensive and very sick, to comfort the Heart very

To perfume Water.

A QUEENS DELIGHT OF Conserves, and Preserves, Candying and Distilling Waters.

To preserve white Pear Plums, or green.

Take the Plums, and cut the stalk off, and wipe them then take the just weight of them in Sugar, then put them in a skillet of water, and let them stand in and scald, being close covered till they be tender, they must not seeth, when they be soft lay them in a Dish, and cover them with a cloth, and stew some of the the Sugar in the glass bottom, and put in the Plums, strewing the sugar over till all be in, then let them stand all night, the next day put them in a pan, and let them boil a pace, keeping them clean scummed, & when your Plums look clear, your syrup will gelly, and they are enough. If your Plums be ripe, peel off the skins before you put them in the glass; they will be the better and clearer a great deal to dry, if you will take the Plums white; if green, do them with the rinds on.

To preserve Grapes

Take Grapes when they be almost through ripe, and cut the stalks off, and stone them in the side, and as fast as you can stone them strew Sugar on them; you must take to every pound of Grapes three quarters of a pound of Sugar, then take some of the sower Grapes; and wring the juyce of them, and put to every pound of Grapes two spoonfuls of juyce, then set them on the fire, and still lift up the pan and shake it round, for fear of burning to, then set them on again, & when the Sugar is melted, boil them as fast as you can possible, and when they look very clear, and the syrup is somewhat thick, they are enough.

To preserve Quinces white.

Take a pair and coar them, and to every pound of your equal weights in Sugar and Quince, take a wine pint of water; put them together, and boil them as fast as you can uncovered; and this way you may also preserve Pippins white as you do Quinces.

To preserve Respass.

Take a pound of Respass, a pound of fine Sugar, a quarter of a pint of the juyce of Respass, strew the Sugar under and above the Respass, sprinkle the juyce all on them, set them on a clear fire, let them boil as soft as is possible, till the syrup will gelly, then take them off, let them stand till they be cold, then put them in a glass. After this manner is the best way.

To preserve Pippins.

Take fair Pippins, and boil them in fair water till they be somewhat tender, then take them out, and peel off the skins and put them into a fair earthen pot, and cover them till they be cold, then make the syrup with fair water and Sugar, seeth it, and scum it very clean, then being almost cold, put in your Pippins, so boil them softly together, put in as much rind of Oranges as you think will tast them, if you have no Oranges take whole Cinamon and Cloves, so boil them high enough to keep them all the year.

To preserve fruits green.

Take Pippins, Apricocks, Pear-Plums, or Peaches when they be green, scald them in hot water, and peel them or scrape them, put them into another water not so hot as the first, then boil them very tender, take the weight of them in Sugar, put to it as much water as will make a syrup to cover them; then boil them something leisurely, and take them up, then boil the syrup till it be somewhat thick, that it will batten on a dish side, and when they are cold, put them together.

To preserve Oranges and Lemons the best way.

Take and boil them as for paste, then take as much sugar as they weigh, and put to it as much water as will cover them by making a syrrup, then boil them very leisurely till they be clear, then take them up and boil the syrup till it batten on the dish side, and when they are cold put them up, &c.

An approved Conserve for a Cough or Consumption of the Lungs.

Take a pound of Elecampane Roots, draw out the pith, and boil them in two waters till they be soft, when it is cold put to it the like quantity of the pap of roasted Pippins, and three times their weight of brown sugar-candy beaten to powder, stamp these in a Mortar to a Conserve, whereof take every morning fasting as much as a Walnut for a week or fortnight together, and afterwards but three times a week. *Approved.*

To make conserve of Any of these Fruits.

When you have boiled your paste as followeth ready to fashion on the Pie-plate, put it up into Gallipots, and never dry it, and this is all the difference between Conserves. And so you may make Conserves of any Fruits, this is for all hard Fruits, as Quinces, Pippins, Oranges and Lemons.

To dry any Fruits after they are preserved, to or Candy them.

Take Pippins, Pears or Plums, and wash them out in warm water from the syrup they are preserved in, strew them over with searsed Sugar, as you would do flower upon fish to fry them; set them in a broad earthen Pan, that they may lie one by one; then set them in a warm Oven or Stove to dry. If you will candy them withall, you must strew on Sugar three or four times in the drying.

To preserve Artichokes young, green Walnuts and Lemons, and the Elecampane-Roots, or any bitter thing.

Take any of these, and boil them tender, and shift them in their boyling six or seven times to take away their bitterness out of one hot water into another, then put a quart of Salt unto them, then take them up and dry them with a fair cloth, then put them into as much clarified Sugar as will cover them, then let them boil a walm or two, and so let them stand soaking in the Sugar till the next morning, then take them up and boil the Sugar a little higher by it self, and when they are cold put them up.

Let your green Walnuts be prickt full of holes with a great pin, and let them not be long in one water, for that will make them look black; being boiled tender, stick two or three Cloves in each of them.

Set your Elecampane-Roots, being clean scraped, and shifted in their boilings a dozen times, then dry them in a fair cloth, and so boil them as is above written, take half so much more than it doth weigh, because it is bitter, &c.

To preserve Quinces white or red.

Take the Quinces, and coar them, and pare them, those that you will have white, put them into a pail of water two or three hours, then take as much Sugar as they weigh, put to it as much water as will make a Syrup to cover them, then boil your Syrup a little while, then put your Quinces in, and boil them as fast as you can, till they be tender and clear, then take them up, and boil the Syrup a little higher by it self, and being cold put them up. And if you will have them red, put them raw into Sugar, and boil them leisurely close covered till they be red and put them not into cold water.

To preserve Grapes.

Take the Clusters, and stone them as you do Barberries, then take a little more Sugar than they weigh, put to it as much Apple water as will make a Syrup to cover them, then boil them as you do Cherries as fast as you can, till the Syrup be thick and being cold pot it, thus may you preserve Barberries or English Currans, or any kind of Berries.

To preserve Pippins, Apricoks, Pear-Plums and Peaches when they are ripe.

Take Pippins and pare them, bore a hole through them, & put them into a Pail of water, then take as much Sugar as they do weigh, and put to it as much water as will make a Syrup to cover them, and boil them as fast as you can, so that you keep them from breaking, until they be tender, that you may prick a Rush through them: let them be a soaking till they be almost cold, then put them up.

Your Apricoks and Peaches must be stoned & pared, but the Pear-Plums must not be stoned nor pared. Then take a little more Sugar than they weigh, then take as much Apple water and Sugar as will make a Syrup for them, then boil them as you do your Pippins, and Pot them as you do the Pippins likewise, &c.

To preserve Pippins, Apricocks, Pear-Plums, or Peaches green.

Take your Pippins green and quoddle them in fair water, but let the water boil first before you put them in, & you must shift them in two hot waters before they will be tender, then pull off the skin from them, and so case them in so much clarified Sugar as will cover them, and so boil them as fast as you can, keeping them from breaking, then take them up, and boil the syrup until it be as thick as for Quiddony; then pot them, and pour the syrup into them before they be cold.

Take your Apricocks and Pear-Plums and boil them tender, then take as much Sugar as they do weigh, and take as much water as will make the syrup, take your green Peaches before they be stoned and thrust a pin through them, and then make a strong water of ashes, and cast them into the hot standing lye to take off the fur from them, then wash them in three or four waters warm, so then put them into so much clarified Sugar as will candy them; so boil them, and put them up, &c.

To dry Pippins, or Pears without Sugar.

Take Pippins or Pears and prick them full of holes with a bodkin, & lay them in sweet wort three or four dayes, then lay them on a sieves bottom, till they be dry in an Oven, but a drying heat. This you may do to any tender Plum.

To make Syrup of Clove-gilly flowers.

Take a quart of water, half a bushel of Flowers, cut off the whites, and with a sieve sift away the seeds, bruise them a little; let your water be boiled, and a little cold again, then put in your Flowers, and let them stand close covered twenty four hours; you may put in but half the flowers at a time, the strength will come out the better; to that liquor put in four pound of Sugar, let it lye in all night, next day boil it in a Gallipot, set it in a pot of water, and there let it boil till all the Sugar be melted and the syrup be pretty thick, then take it out, and let it stand in that till it be through cold, then glass it.

To make Syrup of Hysop for Colds.

Take a handful of Hysop, of Figs, Raisins, Dates, of each an ounce, of Collipint half an handful, French Barley one ounce, boil therein three pints of fair water to a quart, strain it and clarifie it with two whites of Eggs, then put in two pound of fine sugar, and boil it to a syrup.

To make Orange Water.

Take a pottle of the best Maligo Sack, and put in as many of the peels of Oranges as will go in, cut the white clean off, let them steep twenty four hours; still them in a glass still, and let the water run into the Receiver upon fine Sugar-candy; you may still it in an ordinary Still.

To dry Cherries.

Take a pound of sugar, dissolve it in thin fair water, when it is boiled a little while, put in your Cherries after they are stoned, four pound to one pound of Sugar, let them lye in the Sugar three dayes, then take them out of the syrup and lay them on sieves one by one, and set them before the Sun upon stools, turn them every day, else they will mould; when they look of a dark red colour, and are dry then put them up. And so you may do any manner of Fruit. In the Sun is the best drying of them, put into the syrup some juyce of Rasps.

To make juyce of Liquorish.

Take English Liquorish, and stamp it very clean, bruise it with a hammer, and cut it in peices; to a pound of Liquorish thus bruised, put a quart of Hysop water, let them soak together in an earthen pot a day and a night, then pull the Liquorish into small pieces, and lay it in soak again two dayes more; then strain out the Liquorish, and boil the liquor a good while. Stir it often; then put in half a pound of Sugar-candy, or Loaf-sugar finely beaten, four grains of Musk, as much Ambergreece, bruise them small with a little Sugar; then boil them together till it be good & thick, still have care you burn it not; then put it out in glass plates, and make it into round rolls, and set it in a drying place till it be stiff, that you may work it into rolls to be cut as big as Barley corns, and so lay them on a place again: If it be needful strew on the place again a little Sugar to prevent thickning; so dry them still if there be need and if they should be too dry, the heat of the fire will soften them again.

A Perfume for Cloths, Gloves.

Take of Linet two grains, of Musk three, of Ambergreece four, and the oyl of Bems a pretty quantity; grinde them all upon a Marble stone fit for that purpose; then with a brush or sponge rake them over, and it will sweeten them very well; your Gloves or Jerkins must first be washed in red Rose-water, and when they are almost dry, stretch them forth smooth, and lay on the Perfumes.

To make Almond Bisket.

Take the whites of four new laid Eggs, and two yolks, then beat it well for an hour together, then have in readiness a quarter of a pound of the best Almonds blanched in cold water, & beat them very small with Bose-wart, for fear of Oyling; then, have a pound of the best Loaf-sugar finely beaten, beat that in the Eggs a while, then put in your Almonds, and five or six spoonfuls of the finest flower, and so bake them together upon Paper plates, you may have a little fine Sugar in a piece of tiffany to dust them over as they be in the Oven, so bake them as you do Bisket.

To dry Apricocks.

First stone them, then weigh them, take the weight of them in double refined Sugar, make the syrup with so much water as will wet them, and boil it up so high, that a drop being droped on a Plate it will slip clean off, when it is cold, put in your Apricocks being pared, whilst your Syrup is hot, but it must not be taken off the fire before you put them in, then turn them in the syrup often, then let them stand 3 quarters of an hour, then take them out of the syrup, and tie them up in Tiffanies, one in a tiffany or more, as they be in bigness, and whilst you are tying them up, set the syrup on the fire to heat, but not to boil, then put your Apricocks into the syrup, and set them on a quick fire, and let them boil, as fast as you can, skim them clean, and when they look clear take them from the fire, and let them lie in the syrup till the next day, then set them on the fire to heat, but not to boil; then set them by till the next day, and lay them upon a clean Sieve to drain, and when they are well drained, take them out of the Tiffanies, and so dry them in a Stove, or better in the Sun with Glasses over them, to keep them from the dust.

To make Quinces for Pies.

Wipe the Quinces, and put them into a little vessel of swall Beer when it hath done working; stop them close that no air can get in, and this will keep them fair all the year and good.

The best way to break sweet Powder.

Take of Orrice one pound, Calamus a quarter of a pound, Benjamin one half pound, Storax half a pound, Civet a quarter of an ounce, Cloves a quarter of a pound, Musk one half ounce, Oyl of Orange flowers one ounce, Lignum Aloes one ounce, Rosewood a quarter of a pound, Ambergreece a quarter of an ounces. To every pound of Roses put a pound of powder; the bag must be of Taffity, or else the powder will run through.

To make excellent Perfumes.

Take a quarter of a pound of Damask Rose-buds cut clean from the Whites, stamp them very small, put to them a good spoonful of Damask Rose-water, so let them stand close stoopped all night, then take one ounce and a quarter of Benjamin finely beaten, and also searsed, (if you will) twenty grains of Civit, and ten grains of Musk; mingle them well together, then make it up in little Cakes between Rose leaves, and dry them between sheets of Paper.

To make Conserve of Roses boiled.

Take a quart of red Rose-water, a quart of fair water, boil in the Water a pound of red Rose-leaves, the whites cut off, the leaves must be boiled very tender; then take three pound of Sugar, and put to it a pound at a time, and let it boil a little between every pound, so put it up in your pots.

To make Conserves of Roses unboiled.

Take a pound of red Rose leaves, the whites cut off, stamp them very fine, take a pound of Sugar, and beat in with the Roses, and put it in a pot, and cover it with leather, and set it in a cool place.

To make a very good Pomatum.

Take the Fat of a young Dog one pound, it must be killed well that the blood settle not into the fat, then let the outer skin be taken off before it be opened, lest any of the hair come to the fat, then take all the fat from the inside, and as soon as you take it off fling it into Conduit water, and if you see the second skin be clear, peel it and water it with the other: be sure it cools not out of the water: you must not let any of the flesh remain on it, for then the Pomatum will not keep. To one pound of this fat take two pound of Lambs caule, and put it to the other in the water and when you see it is cold, drain it from the water in a Napkin, and break it in little peices with your fingers, and take out all the little veins; then take eight ounces of Oyl of Tartar, and put in that first, stiring it well together, then put it into a Gallon of Conduit water, and let it stand till night; shift this with so much Oyl and Water, morning and evening seven dayes together, and be sure you shift it constantly; and the day before you mean to melt it wring it hard by a little at a time, and be sure the Oyl and water be all out of it, wring the water well out of it with a Napkin every time you shift it; then put in three pints of Rose-water; let it stand close covered twelve hours, then wring out that, and put it in a pint of fresh Rose-water into a high Gallipot with the *Fæces*; then tie it close up, and set it in a pot of water, and let it boil two hours then take it out, and strain it into an earthen Pan, let it stand till it be cold; then cut a hole in it, and let out the water, then scrape away the bottom, and dry it with a cloth, and dry the pan, melt it in a Chafing-dish of Coales, or in the Gallipots; beat it so long till it look very white and shining; then with your hand fling it in fine Cakes upon white paper, and let it lye till it be cold, then put it into Gallipots. This will be very good for two or three years.

To make Raisin Wine.

Take two pound of Raisins of the Sun shred, a pound of good powdered Sugar, the juice of two Lemons, one pill, put these into an earthen Pot with a top, then take two gallons of water, let it boil half an hour, then take it hot from the fire, and put it into the pot, and cover it close for three or four dayes, stirring it twice a day, being strained put it into bottles, and stop it more close, in a fortnight or three weeks it may be drunk; you may put in Clove Gilly flowers, or Cowslips, as the time of the year is when you make it; and when you have drawn this from the Raisins, and bottled it up, heat two quarts of water more, put it to the ingredients, and let it stand as aforesaid. This will be good, but smaller than the other, the water must be boiled as the other.

To make Rasberry Wine.

Take a Gallon of good Rhenish Wine, put into it as much Rasberries very ripe as will make it strong, put it in an earthen pot, and let it stand two dayes, then pour your Wine from your Rasberries, and put into every bottle two ounces of Sugar, stop it up and keep it by you.

The best way to preserve Cherries.

Take the best Cherries you can get, and cut the stalks something short, then for every pound of these Cherries take two pound of other Cherries, and put them of their stalks and stones, put to them ten spoonfuls of fair water, and then set them on the fire to boil very fast till you see that the colour of the syrup be like pale Claret wine, then take it off the fire, and drain them from the Cherries into a Pan to preserve in. Take to every pound of Cherries a quarter of Sugar, of which take half, and dissolve it with the Cherry water drained from the Cherries, and keep them boiling very fast till they will gelly in a spoon, and as you see the syrup thin, take off the Sugar that you kept finely beaten, and put it to the Cherries in the boiling, the faster they boil, the better they will be preserved, and let them stand in a Pan till they be almost cold.

A Tincture of Ambergreece.

Take Ambergreece one ounce, Musk two drams, spirit of Wine half a pint, or as much as will cover the ingredients two or three fingers breadth, put all into a glass, stop it close with a Cork and Bladder; set it in Horse dung ten or twelve days, then pour off gently the Spirit of Wine, and keep it in a Glass close stopt, then put more spirit of Wine on the Ambergreece, and do as before, then pour it off, after all this the Ambergreece will serve for ordinary uses. A drop of this will perfume any thing, and in Cordials it is very good.

To make Usquebath the best way.

Take two quarts of the best *Aqua vitæ*, four ounces of scraped liquorish, and half a pound of sliced Raisins of the Sun, Anniseeds four ounces, Dates and Figs, of each half a pound, sliced Nutmeg, Cinnamon, Ginger, of each half an ounce, put these to the *Aqua vitæ*, stop it very close, and set it in a cold place ten dayes, stirring it twice a day with a stick, then strain and sweeten it with Sugar-candy; after it is strained, let it stand till it be clear, then put into the glass Musk and Ambergreece; two grains is sufficient for this quantity.

To preserve Cherries with a quarter of their weights in Sugar.

Take four pound of Cherries, one pound of Sugar, beat your Sugar and strew a little in the bottom of your skillet, then pull off the stalk and stones of your Cherries, and cut them cross the bottom with a knife; let the juyce of the Cherries run upon the Sugar; for there must be no other liquor but the juyce of the Cherries; cover your Cherries over with one half of your Sugar, boil them very quick, when they are half boiled, put in the remainder of your sugar, when they are almost enough, put in the rest of the sugar; you must let them boil till they part in sunder like Marmalade, stirring them continually; so put them up hot into your Marmalade glasses.

To make Gelly of Pippins.

Take Pippins, and pare them, and quarter them, and put as much water to them as will cover them, and let them boil till all the vertue of the Pippins are out; then strain them, and take to a pint of that liquor a pound of Sugar, and cut long threads of Orange peels, and boil in it, then take a Lemon, and pare and slice it very thin, and boil it in your liquor a little thin, take them out, and lay them in the bottom of your glass, and when it is boiled to a gelly, pour it on the Lemons in the glass. You must boil the Oranges in two or three waters before you boil it in the gelly.

To make Apricock Cakes.

Take the fairest Apricocks you can get, and parboil them very tender, then take off the Pulp and their weight of Sugar, and boil the Sugar and Apricocks together very fast, stir them ever lest they burn to, and when you can see the bottom of the Skillet it is enough; then put then into Cards sowed round, and dust them with fine Sugar, and when they are cold stone them, then turn them, and fill them up with some more of the same stuff; but you must let them stand for three or four dayes before you turn them off the first place; and when you find they begin to candy, take them out of the Cards, dust them with Sugar again; so do ever when you turn them.

To preserve Barberries the best way.

First stone them and weigh them, half a pound of sugar to half a pound of them, then pair them and slice them into that liquor, take the weight of it in sugar; then take as many Rasberries as will colour it, and strain them into the liquor, then put in the sugar, boil it as fast as you can, then skim it till it be very clear, then put in your Barberries, and that sugar you weighed, and so let them boil till the skin be fully risen up, then take them off, and skin them very clean, and put them up.

To make Lozenges of Red Roses.

Boil your sugar to sugar again, then put in your Red Roses being finely beaten and made moist with the juyce of a Lemmon, let it not boil after the Roses are in but pour it upon a Pye-plate, and cut it into what form you please.

To make Chips of Quinces.

First scald them very well, then slice them into a Dish, and pour a Candy Syrup to them scalding hot, and let them stand all night, then lay them on plates, and searse sugar on them, and turn them every day, and scrape more sugar on them till they be dry. If you would have them look clear, heat them in syrup, but not to boil.

To make Sugar of Wormwood, Mint, Anniseed, or any other of that kinde.

Take double refined Sugar, and do but wet it in fair water, or Rose-water and boil it to a Candy, when it is almost boiled take it off, and stir it till it be cold; then drop in three or four drops of the Oyls of whatsoever you will make, and stir it well; then drop it on a board, being before fitted with Sugar.

To make Syrup of Lemons or Citrons.

Pare off all the rindes, then slice your Lemmons very thin, and lay a lare of Sugar finely beaten, and a lare of Lemons in a silver Bason till you have filled it, or as much as you mean to make, & so let it stand all night; the next day pour off the liquor that runs from it into a glass through a Tiffany strainer. Be sure you put sugar enough to them at the first, and it will keep a year good, if it be set up well.

To make Jambals of Apricocks or Quinces.

Take Apricocks or Quinces, and quoddle them tender, then take their Pulp and dry it in a dish over a Chafing-dish of coals, and set it in a Stove for a day or two; then beat it in a stone Mortar, putting in as much Sugar as will make a stiff paste; then colour it with Saunders, Cochinele or blew Starch, and make it up in what colour you please, rowl them with battle doors into long pieces, and tye them up in knots, and so dry them.

To make Cherry-water.

Take nine pound of Cherries, pull out the stones and stalks, break them with you hand, and put them into nine pints of Claret Wine, take nine ounces of Cinamon, and three Nutmegs, bruise them, and put them into this, then take of Rosemary and Balm, of each half a handful, of sweet Marjoram a quarter of a handful; put all these with the aforenamed into an earthen pot well leaded; so let them stand to infuse twenty four hours; so distil it in a Limbeck, keeping the strongest water by it self, put some sugar finely beaten into your glasses. If your first water be too strong, put some of the second to it as you use it. If you please you may tye some Musk and Ambergreese, in a rag, and hang it by a thread in your glass.

To make Orange Cakes.

Take Oranges and pare them as thin as you can, then take out the meats clean, and put them in water; let them lye about an hour, shift the water, and boil them very tender in three or four waters, then put them up, and dry them on a cloath: mince them as small as you can, then put them into a dish, and squeeze all the juyce of the meat into them, and let them stand till the next day, take to every pound of these a pound and a quarter of double refined Sugar. Boil it with a spoonful of water at the bottom to keep it from burning till it be Sugar again; then put in your Oranges and let them stand and dry on the fire, but not boil; then put them on glass plates, and put them in a stove, the next day make them into Cakes, and so fry them as fast as you can.

To preserve Oranges the French way.

Take twelve of the fairest Oranges and best coloured, and if you can get them with smooth skins they are the better, and lay them in Conduit water, six dayes and nights, shifting them into fresh water morning and evening; then boil them very tender, and with a knife pare them very thin, rub them with salt, when you have so done, core them with a coring Iron, taking out the meat and seeds; then rub them with a dry cloth till they be clean, add to every pound of Oranges a pound and half of Sugar, and to a pound of sugar a pint of water; then mingle your, sugar and water well together in a large skillet or pan; beat the whites of three Eggs and put that into it, then set it on the fire, and let it boil till it rises, and strain it through a Napkin; then set it on the fire again, and let it boil till the syrup be thick, then put in your Oranges, and make them seethe as fast as you can, now and then putting in a piece of fine loaf Sugar the bigness of a Walnut, when they have boiled near an hour, put into them a pint of Apple water; then boil them apace, and add half a pint of white Wine, this should be put in before the Apple-water, when your Oranges are very clear, & your Syrup is so thick that it will gelly, (which you may know by setting some to cool in a spoon) when they are ready to be taken off from the fire; then put in the juyce of eight Lemons warm into them, then put them into an earthen pan, and so let them stand till they be cold, then put every Orange in a several glass or pot; if you do but six Oranges at a time it is the better.

To preserve green Plums.

The greatest Wheaten Plum is the best, which will be ripe in the midst of *July*, gather them about that time, or later, as they grow in bigness, but you must not suffer them to turn yellow, for then they never be of good colour; being gathered, lay them in water for the space of twelve hours, and when you gather them, wipe them with a clean linnen cloth, and cut off a little of the stalks of every one, then set two skillets of water on the fire, and when one is scalding hot put in your Plums, and take them from the fire, and cover them, and let them rest for the space of a quarter of an hour; then take them up, and when your other skillet of water doth boil, put them into it; let them but stay in it a very little while, and so let the other skillet of water, wherein they were first boiled, be set to the fire again, and make it to boil, and put in your Plums as before, and then you shall see them rivet over, and yet your Plums very whole; then while they be hot, you must with your knife scrape away the riveting; then take to every pound of Plums a pound and two ounces of Sugar finely beaten, then set a pan with a little fair water on the fire, and when it boils, put in your Plums, and let them settle half a quarter of an hour till you see the colour wax green, then set them off the fire a quarter of an hour, and take a handful of Sugar that is weighed, and strow it in the bottom of the pan wherein you will preserve, and so put in your Plums one by one, drawing the liquor from them, and cast the rest of your Sugar on them; then set the pan on a moderate fire, letting them boil continually but very softly, and in three quarters of an hour they will be ready, as you may perceive by the greenness of your Plums, and thickness of your syrup, which if they be boiled enough, will gelly when it is cold; then take up your Plums, and put them into a Gallipot, but boil your Syrup a little longer, then strain it into some vessel, and being blood-warm, pour it upon your plums, but stop not the pot before they be cold. Note also you must preserve them in such a pan, as they may lye one by another, and turn of themselves; and when they have been five or six days in the syrup, that the syrup grow thin, you may boil it again with a little Sugar, but put it not to your Plums till they be cold. They must have three scaldings, and one boiling.

To dry Plums.

Take three quarters of a pound of Sugar to a pound of black Pear-plums, or Damsins, slit the Plums in the crest, lay a lay of Sugar with a lay of Plums, and let them stand all night; if you stone the Plums, fill up the place with sugar, then boil them gently till they be very tender, without breaking the skins, take them into an earthen or silver dish, and boil your syrup afterwards for a gelly, then pour it on your Plums scalding hot, and let them stand two or three dayes, then let them be put to the Oven after you draw your bread, so often untill your syrup be dryed up, and when you think they are almost dry, lay them in a sieve, and pour some scalding water on them, which will run through the sieve, and set them in an Oven afterwards to dry.

To preserve Cherries the best way, bigger than they grow naturally, &c.

Take a pound of the smallest Cherries, and boil them tender in a pint of fair water, then strain the liquor from the substance, then take two pound of good Cherries, and put them into a preserving-pan with a lay of Cherries, and a lay of sugar: then pour the syrup of the other Cherries about them, and so let them boil as fast as you can with a quick fire, that the syrup may boil over them, and when your syrup is thick and of good colour, then take them up, and let them stand a cooling by partitions one from another, and being cold you may pot them up.

To preserve Damsins, red Plums or black.

Take your Plums newly gathered, and take a little more sugar than they do weigh, then put to it as much water as will cover them; then boil your syrup a little while, and so let it cool, then put in your Damsins or Plums, then boil them leasurely in a pot of seething water till they be tender, then being almost cold pot them up.

To dry Pippins or Pears.

Take your Pippins, Pears, Apricocks, pare them, and lay them in a broad earthen pan one by one, and so rowl them in searsed Sugar as you flower fried fish; put them in an Oven as hot as for manchet, and so take them out, and turn them as long as the Oven is hot; when the Oven is of a drying heat, lay them upon a Paper, and dry them on the bottom of a Sieve; so you may do the least Plum that is.

To dry Pippins or Pears another way.

Take Pippins or Pears, and lay them in an earthen Pan one by one, and when they be baked plump and not broken, then take them out, and lay them upon a Paper, then lay them on a Sieves bottom, and dry them as you did before.

To dry Apricocks tender.

Take the ripest of the Apricoks, pare them, put them into a silver or earthen skillet, and to a pound of Apricocks put three quarters of a pound of Sugar, set your Apricocks over your fire; stirring them till they come to a pulp, and set the Sugar in another skillet by boiling it up to a good height, then take all the Apricocks, and stir them round till they be well mingled, then let it stand till it be something cold and thick, then put it into cards, being cut of the fashion of an Apricock, and laid upon glass plates; fill the Cards half full, then set them in your stove, but when you find they are so dry that they are ready to turn, then provide as much of your pulp as you had before, and so put to every one a stove, when they are turned, (which you must have laid before) & pour the rest of the Pulp upon them, so set them into your stove, turning them till they be dry.

To dry Plums.

Take a pound of Sugar to a pound of Plums, pare them, scald your Plums, then lay your Plums upon a sieve till the water be drained from them, boil your Sugar to a Candy height, and then put your Plums in whilst your syrup is hot, so warm them every morning for a week, then take them out, and put them into your stove and dry them.

To dry Apricocks.

Take your Apricocks, pare and stone them, then weigh half a pound of sugar to a pound of Apricocks, then take half that sugar, and make a thin syrup, and when it boileth, put in the Apricocks; then scald them in that syrup; then take them off the fire, and let them stand all night in that syrup, in the morning take them out of that syrup, and make another syrup with the other half of the sugar, then put them in, and preserve them till they look clear; but be sure you do not do them so much as those you keep preserved without drying; then take them out of that syrup, and lay them on a piece of Plate till they be cold; then take a skillet of fair water, and when the water boils take your Apricocks one after another in a spoon, and dip them in the water first on one side, and then on the other; not letting them go out of the spoon: you must do it very quick, then put them on a piece of plate, and dry them in a Stove, turning them every day; you must be sure that your Stove or Cupboard where you dry them, the heat of it be renewed three times a day with a temperate drying heat untill they be something dry, then afterwards turn once as you see cause.

Conserves of Violets the Italian manner.

Take the leaves of blue Violets separated from their stalks and greens, beat them very well in a stone Mortar, with twice their weight of Sugar, and reserve them for your use in a glass vessel.

The heat of Choller it doth mitigate extinguisheth thirst, asswageth the belly, and helpeth the Throat of hot hurts, sharp droppings and driness, and procureth rest: It will keep one year.

Conserves of red Roses the Italian manner.

Take fresh red Roses not quite ripe, beat them in a stone Mortar, mix them with double their weight of Sugar, and put them in a glass close stopped, being not full, let them remain before you use them three months, stirring of them once a day.

The Vertues.

The Stomach, Heart, and Bowels it cooleth, and hindreth vapours, the spitting of blood and corruption for the most part (being cold) it helpeth. It will keep many years.

Conserve of Borage Flowers after the Italian manner.

Take fresh Borage flowers cleansed well from their heads four ounces, fine sugar twelve ounces, beat them well together in a stone Mortar, and keep them in a vessel well placed.

The vertues are the same with Bugloss flowers.

Conserve of Rosemary flowers after the Italian manner.

Take new Rosemary Flowers one pound, of white sugar one pound; so beat them together in a Marble Mortar with a wooden Pestle, keep it in a gallipot, or vessel of earth well glassed, or in one of hard stone. It may be preserved for one year or two.

The Vertues.

It comforteth the heart, the stomach, the brain, and all the nervous part of the Body.

Conserve of Betony after the Italian way.

Betony new and tender one pound, the best sugar three pound, beat them very small in a stone Mortar, let the sugar be boiled with two pound of Betony-water to the consistance of a syrup, at length mix them together by little and little over a small fire, and make a Conserve, which keep in a glass.

The Vertues.

It helpeth the cold pains of the head, purgeth the stomach and womb: it helpeth stoniness of the Reins, and furthereth Conception.

Conserve of Sage.

Take new flowers of Sage one pound, sugar one pound; so beat them together very small in a Marble Mortar, put them in a vessel well glassed and steeped, set them in the Sun, stir them daily; it will last one year.

The Vertues.

It is good in all cold hurts of the brain, it refresheth the Stomach, it openeth obstructions and takes away superfluous and hurtfull humours from the stomach.

Conserve of flowers of Lavender.

Take the flowers being new, so many as you please, and beat them with three times their weight of white Sugar, after the same manner as Rosemary flowers; they will keep one year.

The Vertues.

The Brain, the Stomach, Liver, Spleen, and Womb it maketh warm, and is good in the Suffocation of the Womb, hardness of the spleen and for the Apoplexy.

Conserve of Marjoram.

The Conserve is prepared as Betony, it keepeth a year.

The Vertues.

It is good against the coldness, moistness of the Brain, and Stomach, and it strengthneth the Vital spirits.

Conserve of Peony after the Italian way.

In the Spring take of the Flowers fresh half a pound, Sugar one pound, beat them together in a good stone Mortar, then put them in a glass, and set them in the sun for three months, stirring them daily with a wooden Spathula.

The Vertues.

It is good against the Falling-sickness, and giddiness in the head, it cleanseth the Reins and Bladder.

Touching Candies, as followeth.

To Candy Rosemary-flowers in the Sun.

Take Gum-Dragon, and steep it in Rose-water, then take the Rosemary flowers, good coloured, and well pickt, and wet them in the water that your Gum dragon is steeped in, then take them out, and lay them upon a paper, and strew fine Sugar over them; this do in the hot sun, turning them, and strewing Sugar on them, till they are candied, and so keep them for your use.

To Make Sugar of Roses.

Take the deepest coloured red Roses, pick them, cut off the white bottoms, and dry your red leaves in an Oven, till they be as dry as possible, then beat them to powder and searse them, then take half a pound of Sugar beaten fine, put it into your pan with as much fair water as will wet it; then set it in a chaffing-dish of coals, and let it boil till it be sugar again, then put as much powder of Roses as will make it look very red stir them well together, and when it is almost cold, put it into pailes, and when it is throughly cold, take them off, and put them in boxes.

To Candy Pippins, Pears, Apricocks or Plums.

Take of these fruits being pared, and strew sugar upon them, as you do flower upon frying fish; then lay them on a board in a Pewter dish, so put them into an Oven as hot as for Manchet; as the liquor comes from them, pour forth, turn them, and strew more Sugar on them, and sprinkle Rose-water on them, thus turning and sugaring of them three or four times, till they be almost dry, then lay them on a Lettice Wire, or on the bottom of a sieve in a warm Oven, after the bread is drawn out, till they be full dry: so you may keep them all the year.

To Candy or clear Rockcandy flowers.

Take spices, and boil them in a syrup of Sugar, then put in the flowers, boil them till they be stiff, when you spread them on a Paper, lay them on round Wires in an earthen pan, then take as much hard Sugar as will fill your pan, and as much water as will melt the sugar, that is half a pint to every pound; then beat a dozen spoonfuls of fair water, and the white of an Egg in a bason, with a birchen rod till it come to a Froth, when your sugar is melted and boiled, put the froth of the Egg in the hot syrup, and as it riseth, drop in a little cold water; so let it boil a little while, then scum it, then boil it to a Candy height, that is, when you may draw it in small threads between your finger and your thumb: then pour forth all your syrup that will run from it in your pan, then set it a drying one hour or two, which done pick up the wiers, and take off the flowers, and lay them on papers, and so dry them.

To Candy Spanish Flowers.

Take the Blossoms of divers sorts of flowers, and make a syrup of water and sugar, and boil it very thick, then put in your Blossoms, and stir them in their boiling, till it turn to sugar again, then stir them with the back of a spoon, till the Sugar fall from it; so may you keep them for Sallets all the year.

To Candy Grapes, Cherries or Barberries.

Take of these fruits, and strew fine sifted sugar on them, as you do flower on frying fish, lay them on a lattice of wier in a deep earthen pan, and put them into an Oven as hot as for Manchet; then take them out, and turn them and sugar them again, and sprinkle a little Rose-water on them, pour the syrup forth as it comes from them, thus turning and sugaring them till they be almost dry, then take them out of the earthen pan, and lay them on a lattice of wire, upon two billets of wood in a warm Oven, after the bread is drawn, till they be dry and well candied.

To Candy Suckets of Oranges, Lemons, Citrons, and Angelica.

Take, and boil them in fair water tender, and shift them in three boilings, six or seven times, to take away their bitterness, then put them into as much Sugar as will cover them, and so let them boil a walm or two, then take them out, and dry them in a warm Oven as hot as Manchet, and being dry boil the Sugar to a Candy height, and so cast your Oranges into the hot Sugar, and take them out again suddenly, and then lay them upon a lattice of Wyer or the bottom of a Sieve in a warm Oven after the bread is drawn, still warming the Oven till it be dry, and they will be well candied.

To Candy the Orange Roots.

Take the Orange Roots being well and tenderly boiled, petch them and peel them, and wash them out of two or three waters; then dry them well with a fair cloth; then pot them together two or three in a knot, then put them into as much clarified Sugar as will cover them, and so let them boil leisurely, turning them well until you see the Sugar drunk up into the Root; then shake them in the Bason to sunder the knits; and when they wax dry, take them up suddenly, and lay them on sheets of white Paper, and so dry them before the fire an hour or two, and they will be candied.

Candy Orange Peels after the Italian way.

Take Orange Peels so often steeped in cold water, as you think convenient for their bitterness, then dry them gently, and candy them with some convenient syrup made with Sugar, some that are more grown, take away that spongious white under the yellow peels, others do both together.

The Vertues.

They corroborate the Stomach and Heart.

To Candy Citrons after the Spanish way.

Take Citron Peels so large as you please the inner part being taken away, let them be steeped in a clear lye of water and ashes for nine dayes, and shift them the fifth day, afterward wash them in fair water, till the bitterness be taken away, and that they grow sweet, then let them be boiled in fair water till they grow soft, the watry part being taken away, let them be steeped in a vessel of stone twenty four hours, with a Julip, made of white Sugar and three parts water; after let them be boiled upon a gentle fire, to candiness of Penidies or Paste; being taken out of that, let them be put into a glass vessel, one by one, with the julip of Roses made somewhat hard or with sugar; some do add Amber and Musk to them.

The Vertues.

It comforteth the Stomach and Heart, it helpeth concoction.

Candied Cherries, the Italian way.

Take Cherries before they are full ripe, the stones taken out, put clarified sugar boiled to a height, then pour it on them.

Chicory Roots candied the Italian way.

Take Chicory new and green, the outward Bark being taken away, then before they be candied, let them be cut in several parts, and gently boiled, that no bitterness may remain, then set them in the air placed severally, and put sugar to them boiled to a height.

Touching Marmalets, and Quiddony, as followeth.

To make Marmalet of Damsins.

Take two quarts of Damsins that be through ripe, and pare off the skin of three pints of them, then put them into an earthen Pipkin, those with the skins undermost then set the Pipkin into a pot of seething water, and let the water seethe apace untill the Damsins be tender. Cover the Pipkin close, that no water gets into them, and when they are tender, put them out into an earthen pan, and take out all the stones and skins, and weigh them, and take the weight with hard sugar, then break the sugar fine, and put it into the Damsins, then set it on the fire, and make it boil apace till it will come from the bottome of the skillet, then take it up, and put it into a glass but scum it clear in the boiling.

To make white Marmalet of Quinces.

Take unpared Quinces, and boil them whole in fair water, peel them and take all the pap from the core, to every pound thereof add three quarters of a pound of Sugar, boil it well till it comes well from the pans bottom, then put it into boxes.

To make Marmalet of any tender Plum.

Take your Plums, & boil them between two dishes on a Chafing dish of coals, then strain it, and take as much Sugar as the Pulp doth weigh, and put to it as much Rose-water, and fair water as will melt it, that is, half a pint of water to a pound of Sugar, and so boil it to a Candy height, then put the pulp into hot sugar, with the pap of a roasted apple. In like manner you must put roasted apples to make Past Royal of it, or else it will be tough in the drying.

To make Orange Marmalet.

Take Oranges, pare them as thin as you can; boil them in four several waters, let them be very soft before you take them out, then take two quarts of Spring-water, put thereto twenty Pippins pared, quartered, and coared, let them boil till all the vertue be out, take heed they do not lose the colour; then strain them, put to every pint of water a pound of sugar, boil it almost to a Candy-height, then take out all the meat out of the Oranges, slice the peel in long slits as thin as you can, then put in your peel with the juyce of two Lemmons, and one half Orange, then boil it to a Candy.

To make Quiddony of Pippins of Ruby or any Amber colour.

Take Pippins, and cut them in quarters, and pare them, and boil them with as much fair water as will cover them, till they be tender, and sunk into the water, then strain all the liquor from the Pulp, then take a pint of that liquor, and half a pound of Sugar, and boil it till it be a quaking gelly on the back of a spoon; so then pour it on your moulds, being taken out of fair water; then being cold turn them on a wet trencher, and so slide them into the boxes, and if you would have it ruddy colour, then boil it leasurely close covered, till it be as red as Claret Wine, so may you conceive, the difference is in the boiling of it; remember to boil your Quinces in Apple-water as you do your Plums.

To make Quiddony of all kind of Plums.

Take your Apple-water, and boil the Plums in it till it be red as Claret Wine, and when you have made it strong of the Plums, put to every pint half a pound of Sugar, and so boil it till a drop of it hang on the back of a spoon like a quaking gelly. If you will have it of an Amber colour, then boil it with a quick fire, that is all the difference of the colouring of it.

To make Marmalet of Oranges, or Orange Cakes, &c.

Take the yellowest and fairest Oranges, and water them three days, shifting the water twice a day, pare them as thin as you possible can, boil them in a water changed five or six times, until the bitterness of the Orange be boiled out, those that you preserve must be cut in halves, but those for Marmalet must be boiled whole, let them be very tender, and slice them very thin on a Trencher, taking out the seeds and long strings, and with a Knife make it as fine as the Pap of an Apple; then weigh your Pap of Oranges, and to a pound of it, take a pound and a half of sugar; then you must have Pippins boiled ready in a skillet of fair water, and take the pap of them made fine on a Trencher, and the strings taken out, (but take not half so much Pippins as Oranges) then take the weight of it in sugar, and mix it both together in a Silver or Earthen Dish; and set it on the coals to dry the water out of it, (as you do with Quince Marmalet) when your sugar is Candy height, put in your stuff, and boil it till you think it stiff enough, stirring it continually: if you please you may put a little Musk in it.

Touching Pastrey and Pasties.

To make Sugar Cakes.

Take three pound of the finest Wheat Flower, one pound of fine Sugar, Cloves, and Mace of each one ounce finely searsed, two pound of butter, a little Rose-water, knead and mould this very well together, melt your butter as you put it in; then mould it with your hand forth upon a board, cut them round with a glass, then lay them on papers, and set them in an Oven, be sure your Oven be not too hot, so let them stand till they be coloured enough.

To make clear Cakes of Plums.

Take Plums of any sorts, Raspiss are the best, put them in a stone Jug, into a pot of seething water, and when they are dissolved, strain them together through a fair cloth, and take to a pint of that a pound of sugar, put to as much color as will melt it, and boil to a Candy height; boil the liquor likewise in another Posnet, then put them seething hot together, and so boil a little while stirring them together, then put them into glasses, and set them in an Oven or Stove in a drying heat, let them stand so two or three weeks, and never be cold, removing them from one warm place to another, they will turn in a week; beware you set them not too hot, for they will be tough; so every day turn them till they be dry; they will be very clear.

To make Paste of Oranges and Lemons.

Take your Oranges well coloured, boil them tender in water, changing them six or seven times in the boiling, put into the first water one handful of Salt, and then beat them in a wooden bowl with a wooden Pestle, and then strain them through a piece of Cushion Canvas, then take somewhat more than the weight of them in Sugar, then boil it, dry and fashion it as you please.

To make Rasberry Cakes.

Take Rasberries, and put them into a Gallipot, cover them close, and set them into a skillet of water, and let them boil till they are all to mash, then rub them through a strainer of Cushion Canvas, put the liquor into a silver bason, and set it upon a very quick fire; and put into it one handful or two of whole Rasberries, according to the quantity of your liquor; and as you shall like to have seeds in your paste: Thus let it boyl very fast till it be thick; and continually stir, lest it burn; then take two silver dishes that are of a weight, and put them into your scales, in the one put the Raspiss stuffe, and in the other double refined Sugar finely beaten, as much as the weight of Raspiss stuff; then put as much water to the sugar as will melt it, set it upon the fire, and let it boil till it be very high candied, then take it from the fire, and put your Raspiss stuff into it; and when your Sugar and Rasberries are very well mixt together, and the sugar well melted from about the dish, (which if it will not do from the fire, set it on again) but let it not boil in any case; when it is pretty cool, lay it by spoonfuls in places, and put it into your stuff, keeping temperate fire to it twice a day till it be candied that will turn them, joyn two of the pieces together, to make the cakes the thicker.

To make Paste of Genoa Citrons.

Take Citrons, & boil them in their skins, then scrape all the pulp from the core, strain it through a piece of Cushion Canvas, take twice the weight of the pulp in Sugar, put to it twice as much water as will melt it that is half a pint to every pound of Sugar, boil it to a Candy height; dry the Pulp upon a Chafing-dish of Coales, then put the syrup and the Pulp hot together, boil it with stirring until it will lye upon a Pye-plate, set it in a warm stone Oven upon two billets of wood, from the heat of the Oven, all one night, in the morning turn it, and set it in the like heat again, so turn it every day till it be dry.

To make a French Tart.

Take a quarter of Almonds or thereabouts, and peel them, then beat them in a mortar, take the white of the breast of a cold Capon, and take so much

Lard as twice the quantity of the Capon, and so much Butter, or rather more, and half a Marrow-bone, and if the bone be little then all the Marrow, with the juyce of one Lemon; beat them all together in a Mortar very well, then put in one half pound of loaf sugar grated, then take a good piece of Citron, cut it in small pieces, and half a quarter of Pistanius, mingle all these together, take some flour, and the yolks of two or three Eggs, and some sweet Butter, and work it with cold water.

To make Cakes of Pear Plums.

Take a pound of the clear, or the Pulp, a pound of Sugar, and boil it to a Sugar again, then break it as small as you can, and put in the clear, when your Sugar is melted in it, and almost cold, put it in glass plates, and set them into your stove as fast as you can, with coals under them, and so twice a day whilst they be dry enough to cut; if you make them of the clear, you must make paste of Apples to lay upon them, you must scald them, and beat them very well, and so use them as you do your Plums, and then you may put them into what fashion you please.

To make Cakes, viz.

Take a pound of Sugar finely beaten, four yolks of Eggs, two whites, one half pound of Butter washt in Rose-water, six spoonfuls of sweet Cream warmed, one pound of Currans well pickt, as much flower as will make it up, mingle them well together, make them into Cakes, bake them in an Oven; almost as hot as for Manchet, half an hour will bake them.

To make a Cake the way of the Royal Princess, the Lady Elizabeth, daughter to King Charles the first.

Take half a peck of Flower, half a pint of Rose-water, a pint of Ale-yeast, a pint of Cream, boil it, a pound and an half of Butter, six Eggs, (leave out the whites) four pound of Currans, one half pound of Sugar, one Nutmeg, and a little Salt, work it very well, and let it stand half an hour by the fire, and then work it again, and then make it up, and let it stand an hour and a half, in the Oven; let not your Oven be too hot.

To make Paste of Apricocks.

Take your Apricock, & pare them, and stone them, then boil them tender betwixt two dishes on a Chafing-dish of coals; then being cold, lay it forth on a white sheet of paper; then take as much sugar as it doth weigh, & boil it to a candy height, with as much Rose-water and fair water as will melt the sugar; then put the pulp into the Sugar, and so let it boil till it be as thick as for Marmalet, now and then stirring of it; then fashion it upon a Pye-plate like to half Apricocks, and the next day close the half Apricocks to the other, and when they are dry, they will be as cleer as Amber, and eat much better than Apricocks itself.

To make Paste of Pippins like leaves, and some like Plums, with their stones, and Stalks in them.

Take Pippins pared and coared, and cut in pieces, and boiled tender, so strain them, and take as much Sugar as the Pulp doth weigh, and boil it to a Candy height with as much Rose-water and fair water as will melt it, then put the pulp into the hot sugar, and let it boil until it be as thick as Marmalet; then fashion it on a Pye-plate, like Oaken leaves, and some like half Plums, the next day close the half Plums together; and if you please you may put the stones and stalks in them, and dry them in an Oven, and if you will have them look green, make the paste when Pippins are green; and if you would have them look red, put a little Conserves of Barberries in the Paste, and if you will keep any of it all the year, you must make it as thin as Tart stuff, and put it into Gallipots.

To make Paste of Elecampane roots, an excellent remedy for the Cough of the Lungs.

Take the youngest Elecampane roots, and boil them reasonably tender; then pith them and peel them; and so beat it in a Mortar, then take twice as much sugar as the Pulp doth weigh, and so boil it to a Candy height, with as much Rose-water as will melt it; then put the pulp into the Sugar with the pap of a roasted-apple, then let it boil till it be thick, then drop it on a Pye-plate, and so dry it in an Oven till it be dry.

To make Paste of flowers of the colour of Marble, tasting of natural flowers.

Take every sort of pleasing Flowers, as Violets, Cowslips, Gilly-flowers, Roses or Marigolds, and beat them in a Mortar, each flower by it self with sugar, till the sugar become the colour of the flower, then put a little Gum Dragon steept in water into it, and beat it into a perfect paste; and when you have half a dozen colours, every flower will take of his nature, then rowl the paste therein, and lay one piece upon another, in mingling sort, so rowl your Paste in small rowls, as big and as long as your finger, then cut it off the bigness of a small Nut, overthwart, and so rowl them thin, that you may see a knife through them, so dry them before the fire till they be dry.

To make Paste of Rasberries or English Currans.

Take any of the Frails, and boil them tender on a Chafing-dish of coals betwixt two dishes and strain them, with the pap of a rosted Apple; then take as much sugar as the Pulp doth weigh, and boil to a Candy height with as much Rose-water as will melt it; then put the Pulp into the hot Sugar, and let it boil leisurely till you see it is as thick as Marmalet, then fashion it on a Pie-plate, and put it into the Oven with two billets of wood, that the place touch not the bottom, and so let them dry leasurely till they be dry.

To make Naples Bisket.

Take of the same stuff the Mackaroons are made of, and put to it an ounce of pine-apple-seeds in a quarter of a pound of stuff, for that is all the difference between the Mackaroons and the Naples Bisket.

To make Italian Biskets.

Take a quarter of a pound of searsed sugar, and beat it in an Alablaster mortar with the white of an Egg, and a little Gum Dragon steept in Rose-water, to bring it to a perfect paste, then mould it up with a little Anniseed and a grain of Musk; then make it up like Dutch-bread, and bake it on a Pie-plate in a warm Oven till they rise somewhat high and white, take them out, but handle them not till they be throughly dry and cold.

To make Prince Biskets

Take a pound of searsed sugar, and a pound of fine flower, eight Eggs with two of the reddest yolks taken out, and so beat together one whole hour, then take you Coffins, and indoice them over with Butter very thin, then put an ounce of Anniseeds finely dusted, and when you are ready to fill your Coffins, put in the Anniseeds and so bake it in an Oven as hot as for Manchet.

To make Marchpane to Ice and Gild, and garnish it according to Art.

Take Almonds, and blanch them out of seething water, and beat them till they come to a fine paste in a stone Mortar, then take fine searsed sugar, and so beat it altogether till it come to a prefect paste, putting in now and then a spoonful of Rose-water, to keep it from oyling; then cover your Marchpane with a sheet of paper as big as a Charger, then cut it round by that Charger, and set an edge about it as about a Tart, then bottom it with Wafers, then bake it in an Oven, or in a Baking-pan, and when it is hard and dry, take it out of the Oven, and ice it with Rose-water and Sugar, and the white of an Egg, being as thick as butter, and spread it over thin with two or three feathers; and then put it into the Oven again, and when you see it rise high and white, take it out again and garnish it with some pretty conceit, and stick some long Comfits upright in it, so gild it, then strow Biskets and Carrawayes on it. If your Marchpane be Oyly in beating, then put to it as much Rose-water as will make it almost as thin as to ice.

Lozenges

Take Blossoms of Flowers, and beat them in a bowl-dish, and put them in as much clarified Sugar as may come to the colour of the cover, then boile them with stirring, till it is come to Sugar again; then beat it fine, and searse it, and so work it up to paste with a little Gum Dragon, steep it in Rose-water, then print it with your mould, and being dry, keep it up.

To make Walnuts artificial.

Take searsed Sugar, and Cinnamon, of quantity a like, work it up with a little Gum Dragon, steep it in Rose-water, and print it in a mould made like a Walnut-shell, then take white Sugar Plates, print it in a mold made like a Walnut kernel, so when they are both dry, close them up together with a little Gum Dragon betwixt, and they will dry as they lie.

To make Collops like Bacon of Marchpane.

Take some of your Marchpane Paste, and work it in red Saunders till it be red; then rowl a broad sheet of white Paste, and a sheet of red Paste, three of the white, and four of the red, and so one upon another in mingled sorts, every red between, then cut it overthwart, till it look like Collops of Bacon, then dry it.

To make artificial Fruits.

Take a Mould made of Alablaster, three yolks, and tye two pieces together, and lay them in water an hour, and take as much sugar as will fill up your mold, and boil it in a *Manus Christi*, then pour it into your mould suddenly, and clap on the lid, round it about with your hand, and it will be whole and yellow, then colour it with what colour you please, half red, or half yellow, and you may yellow it with a little Saffron steept in water.

Touching Preserves and Pomanders.

To make an excellent perfume to burn between two Rose leaves.

Take an ounce of Juniper, an ounce of Storax, half a dozen drops of the water of Cloves, six grains of Musk, a little Gum Dragon steept in water, and beat all this to paste, then roll it in little pieces as big as you please, then put them betwixt two Rose-leaves, and so dry them in a dish in an Oven, and being so dried, they will will burn with a most pleasant smell.

To make Pomander.

Take an ounce of Benjamin, an ounce of Storax, and an ounce of Laudanum, heat a Mortar very hot, and beat all these Gums to a perfect paste; in beating of it, put in six grains of Musk, four grains of Civet; when you have beaten all this to a fine paste with you hands with Rose-water, rowl it round betwixt your hands, and make holes in the heads, and so string them while they be hot.

To make an Ipswich Water.

Take a pound of fine white Castle-soap shave it thin in a pint of Rose-water, and let it stand two or three days; then pour all the water from it, and put to it half a pint of freshwater; and so let it stand one whole day, then pour out that, and put half a pint more, and let it stand a night more then put to it half an ounce of powder called sweet Marjoram, a quarter of an ounce of the powder of Winter-Savory, two or three drops of the Oyl of Spike, and the Oyl of Cloves, three grains of Musk, and as much Ambergreese; work all these together in a fair Mortar, with the powder of an Almond Cake dryed, and beaten as small as fine flour, so rowl it round in your hands in Rose-water.

To make a sweet Smell.

Take the Maste of a sweet Apple-tree, being gathered betwixt the two Lady-dayes, and put to it a quarter of Damask Rose-water, & dry it in a dish in an Oven; wet in drying two or three times with Rose-water, then put to it an ounce of Benjamin, an ounce of Storax Calamintæ: these Gums being beaten to powder, with a few leaves of Roses, then you may put what cost of Smells you will bestow, as much Civet or Ambergreese, and beat it altogether in a Pomander or a Bracelet.

Touching Wine.

To make Hypocras.

Take four Gallons of Claret Wine, eight ounces of Cinnamon, three Oranges, of Ginger, Cloves, and Nutmegs a small quantity, Sugar six pound, three sprigs of Rosemary, bruise all the spices somewhat small, and so put them into the Wine, and keep them close stopped, and often shaked together a day or two, then let it run through a gelly bag twice or thrice with a quart of new Milk.

The Lady Thornburghs Syrup of Elders.

Take Elder-berries when they be red, bruise them in a stone Mortar, strain the juyce, and boil it to a consumption of almost half, scum it very clear, take it off the fire whilest it is hot, put in sugar to the thickness of a syrup; put it no more on the fire, when it is cold, put it into Glasses, not filling them to the top, for it will work like Beer.

This cleanseth the stomach and spleen, and taketh away all obstructions of the Liver, by taking the quantity of a spoonful in a morning, and fasting a short time after it.

To make gelly of Raspis the best way.

Take the Raspis, and set them over the fire in a Posnet, and gather out the thin juyce, the bottom of the skillet being cooled with fair water, and strain it with a fine strainer, and when you have as much as you will, then weigh it with Sugar, and boil them till they come to a Gelly, which you may perceive by drawing your finger on the back of the spoon.

To dry Fox Skins.

Take your shee Fox Skins, nail them upon a board as strait as you can, then brush them as clean as you can, then take Aqua Fortis, and put into it a six pence, and still put in more as long as it will dissolve it, then wash your skin over with this water, and set it to dry in the sun; and when it is dry, wash it over with the spirits of wine; this must be done in hottest time of Summer.

Choice Secrets made known.

To make true Magistery of Pearl.

Dissolve two or three ounces of fine seed Pearl in distilled Vinegar, & when it is perfectly dissolved, and all taken up, pour the Vinegar into a clean glass Bason; then drop some few drops of Oyl of Tartar upon it, & it will cast down the Pearl into fine Powder, then pour the Vinegar clean off softly, then put to the Pearl clear Conduit or Spring water; pour that off, and do so often untill the taste of the Vinegar and Tartar be clean gone, then dry the powder of Pearl upon warm embers, and keep it for your use.

How to make Hair grow.

Take half a pound of Aqua Mellis in the Spring time of the year, warm a little of it every Morning when you rise in a Sawcer, and tie a little spunge to a fine box comb, and dip it in the water, and therewith moisten the roots of the Hair in combing it, and it will grow long, thick, and curled in a very short time.

To write Letters of Secret, that they cannot be read without the directions following.

Take fine Allum, beat it small, and put a reasonable quantity of it into water, then write with the said water.

The work cannot be read, but by steeping your paper in fair running water.

You may likewise write with Vinegar, or the juyce of Lemon or Onion; if you would read the same, you must hold it before the fire.

How to keep Wine from Sowring.

Tye a piece of very salt Bacon on the inside of your barrel, so as it touch not the Wine, which will preserve Wine from sowring.

To take out Spots of Grease or Oyl.

Take bones of sheeps feet, burn them almost to ashes, then bruise them to powder, and put of it on the spot, and lay it in the sun when it shineth hottest, when the powder becomes black, lay on fresh in the place till it fetch out the spots, which will be done in a very short time.

To make hair grow black, though any colour.

Take a little Aqua Fortis, put therein a groat or sixpence, as to the quantity of the aforesaid water, then set both to dissolve before the fire, then dip a small spunge in the said water, and wet your beard or hair therewith; but touch not the skin.

King Edwards perfume.

Take twelve spoonfuls of right red Rose-water, the weight of six pence in fine powder of Sugar, and boil it on hot Embers and Coles softly, and the house will smell as though it were full of Roses; but you must burn the sweet Cypress wood before, to take away the gross air.

Queen Elizabeths Perfume.

Take eight spoonfuls of Compound water, the weight of two pence in fine powder of Sugar, and boil it on hot Embers and Coals, softly, and half an ounce of sweet Marjoram dried in the Sun, the weight of two pence of the powder of Benjamin. This Perfume is very sweet, and good for the time.

Mr. Ferene of the New Exchange, Perfumer to the Queen, his rare Dentifrice, so much approved of at Court.

First take eight ounces of Ireos roots, also four ounces of Pomistone, and eight ounces of Cutle-bone, also eight ounces of Corral, and a pound of Brick if you desire to make them red; but he did oftener make them white, and then instead of the Brick did take a pound of fine Alabaster; all this being throughly beaten, and sifted through a fine searse, the powder is then ready prepared to make up in a paste, which must be done as follows.

To make the said Powder into Paste.

Take a little Gum Dragant, and lay it in steep twelve hours, in Orange flower water, or Damask Rose-water, and when it is dissolved, take the sweet Gum, and grind it on a Marble stone with the aforesaid powder, and mixing some crums of white bread, it will come into a Paste, the which you may make Dentifrices, of what shape or fashion you please, but rolls is the most commodious for your use.

The Receipt of the Lady Kents powder, presented by her Ladyship to the Queen.

Take white Amber, Crabs eyes, red Corral, Harts-horn and Pearl, all prepared several, of each a like proportion, tear and mingle them, then take Harts-horn gelly, that hath some Saffron put into a bag, dissolve into it while the gelly is warm, then let the gelly cool, and therewith make a paste of the powders, which being made up into little balls, you must dry gently by the fire side. Pearl is prepared by dissolving it with the juyce of Lemons, Amber prepared by beating it to powder; so also Crabs-eyes and Coral, Harts-horn prepared by burning it in the fire, and taking the shires of it especially, the pith wholly rejected.

A Cordial Water of Sir Walter Raleigh.

Take a gallon of Strawberries, and put them into a pint of *Aqua vitæ*, let them stand for four or five days, strain them gently out, and sweeten the water as you please with fine Sugar; or else with perfume.

The Lady Malets Cordial Water.

Take a pound of fine Sugar beaten and put to it a quart of running water, pour it three or four times through a bag; then put a pint of Damask Rose-water, which you must always pour still through the bag, then four penniworth of Angelica water, four pence in Clove-water, four pence of Rosa Solis, one pint of Cinnamon-water, or three pints and a half *Aqua vitæ*, as you find it in taste; put all these together three or four times through the bag or strainer, and then take half an ounce of good Muskallis and cut them grosly, & put them into a glass, and fill them with the water, &c.

A Sovereign Water of Dr. Stephens, *which he long times used, wherewith he did many Cures; he kept secretly till a little before his death, and then he gave it to the Lord Arch-bishop of* Canterbury *in writing, being as followeth, viz.*

Take a Gallon of good Gascoine Wine, and take Ginger, Gallingale, Cinamon, Nutmegs, Cloves, Grains, Anniseeds, Fennil-seed, of every of them a dram, then take Caraway-seed, of red Mints, Roses, Thime, Pellitory of the Wall, Rosemary, wild Thime, Camomil, the leaves if you cannot get the flowers, of small Lavander, of each a handful, then bray the Spices small, and bray the Herbs, and put all into the Wine, and let it stand for twelve hours, stirring divers times, then still it in a Limbeck, and keep the first water, for it is best, then put the second water by it self, for it is good, but not of such vertues, &c.

The Vertues of this water.

It comforts the Spirits Vital, and helps all inward Diseases that come of cold, it is good against the shaking of the Palsie; it cures the contraction of the Sinews, helps the conception of Women if they be Barren, it kills the Worms in the Belly and Stomach; it cures the cold Dropsie, and helps the Stone in the Bladder, and in the Reins of the back; it helps shortly the stinking breath, and whosoever useth this Water morning and evening, (and not too often) it preserveth him in good liking, and will make him seem young very long, and Comforteth nature marvellously; with this water did Dr. *Stephens* preserve his life, till extream age would not let him go or stand

and he continued five years, when all the Physicians judged he would not live a year longer, nor did he use any other Medicine but this, &c.

A Plague Water to be taken one spoonful every four hours with one sweat every time.

Take Scabious; Betony, Pimpernel, and Turmentine-roots, of each a pound, steep these all night in three gallons of strong Beer, and distil them all in a Limbeck, and when you use it, take a spoonful thereof every four hours, and sweat well after it, draw two quarts of water, if your Beer be strong, and mingle them both together.

Poppy water.

Take four pound of the flower of Poppies well pickt and sifted, steep them all night in three Gallons of Ale that is strong, and still it in a Limbeck; you may draw two quarts, the one will be strong and the other will be small, &c.

A Water for a Consumption, or for a Brain that is weak.

Take Cream (or new milk) and Claret-wine, of each three pints of Violet-flowers, Bugloss and Borage-flowers, of each a spoonful, Comfrey, Knot-grass, and Plantane of these half a handful, three or four Pome-waters sliced, a stick of Liquorish, some Pompion seeds and strings; put to this a Cock that hath been chased and beaten before he was killed, dress it as to boil, and parboil it until there be no blood in it; then put them in a pot, and set them over your Limbeck, and the soft fire; draw out a pottle of water, then put your water in a Pipkin over a Charcoal fire, and boil it a while, dissolve therein six ounces of white Sugar-candy, & two penny weight of Saffron: when it is cold strain it into a glass, & let the Patient drink three or four spoonfuls three or four times a day blood-warm; your Cock must be cut into small pieces, & the bones broken, and in case the flowers and herbs are hard to come by, a spoonful of their stilled waters are to be used.

Another of the same.

Take a pottle of good Milk, one pint of Muscadine, half a pint of red Rose-water, a penny manchet sliced thin, two handfuls of Raisins of the sun stoned, a quarter of a pound of fine sugar, sixteen Eggs beaten; mix all these together, then distill them in a common still with a soft fire, then let the Patient drink three or four spoonfuls at a time blood warm, being sweetned with *Manus Christi* made with Corral and Pearl; when your things are all in the still, strew four ounces of Cinamon beaten; this water is good to put into broath, &c.

A good Stomach Water.

Take a quart of *Aqua Composita*, or *Aqua vitæ*, (the smaller) and put into it one handful of Cowslip flowers, a good handful of Rosemary flowers, sweet Marjoram, a little Pellitory of the Wall, a little Betony and Balm, of each a little handful, Cinnamon half an ounce, Nutmegs a dram, Anniseeds, Coriander seeds, Caroway seeds, Gromel seeds, Juniper berries, of each a dram, bruise the spice and seed, and put them into *Aqua Composita*, or *Aqua vitæ*, with your Herbs together, and put into them a pound of very fine sugar, stir them well together, and put them into a glass and let it stand in the sun nine days, and stir it every day; two or three Dates, and a little race of Ginger sliced into it will make it the better, especially against wind, &c.

A Bag of purging Ale.

Take of Agrimony, Speedwell, Liverwort, Scurvy-grass, Water cresses, of each a handful, of Monks Rhubarb, and red Madder, of each half a pound, of Horseradishes three ounces, Liquorish two ounces, Sassafrage four ounces, Sena seven ounces, sweet Fennil-seeds two drams, Nutmegs four; pick and wash your Herbs and Roots, and bruise them in a Mortar, and put them in a bag made of a Bolter, & so hang them in three gallons of middle Ale, and let it work in the Ale, and after three days you may drink it as you see occasion, &c.

The Ale of Health and Strength, by Viscount St. Albans.

Take Sassafras wood half an ounce, Sarsaparilla three ounces, white Saunders one ounce, Chamapition an ounce, China-root half an ounce, Mace a quarter of an ounce, cut the wood as thin as may be with a knife into small peices, and bruise them in a Mortar; put to them these sorts of Herbs, (viz.) Cowslip flowers, Roman-wormwood, of each a handful, of Sage, Rosemary, Betony, Mugwort, Balm and Sweet-marjoram, of each half a handful, of Hops; boil all these in six gallons of Ale till it come to four; then put the wood and hearbs into six gallons of Ale of the second wort, and boil it till it come to four, let it run from the dregs, and put your Ale together, and tun it as you do other purging Ale, &c.

A Water excellent good against the Plague.

Take three pints of Malmsey, or Muscadine, of Sage and Rue, of each one handful, boil them together gently to one pint, then strain it and set it on the fire again, and put to it one penniworth of Long Pepper, Ginger four drams, Nutmegs two drams, all beaten together, then let it boil a little, take it off the fire, and while it is very hot, dissolve therein six penniworth of Mithridate, and three penniworth of Venice Treacle, and when it is almost cold put to it a pint of strong Angelica water, or so much *Aqua vitæ*, and so keep it in a glass close stopped.

A Cordial Cherry-water.

Take a pottle of *Aqua vitæ*, two ounces of ripe Cherries stoned, Sugar one pound, twenty four Cloves, one stick of Cinamon, three spoonfuls of aniseeds bruised, let these stand in the *Aqua vitæ* fifteen days, and when the water hath fully drawn out the tincture, pour it off into another glass for your use, which keep close stopped, the Spice and the Cherries you may keep, for they are very good for winde in the Stomach.

The Lord Spencers Cherry-water.

Take a pottle of new Sack, four pound of through ripe Cherries stoned, put them into an earthen pot, to which put an ounce of Cinnamon, Saffron unbruised one dram, tops of Balm, Rosemary or their flowers, of each one handful, let them stand close covered twenty four hours, now and then stirring them; then put them into a cold Still, to which put of beaten Amber two drams, Corianderseed one ounce, Alkerms one dram, and distill it leisurely, and when it is fully distilled, put to it twenty grains of Musk. This is an excellent Cordial, good for Faintings and Swoundings, for the Crudities of the Stomach, Winde and Swelling of the Bowels, and divers other evil Symptomes in the Body of Men and Women.

The Herbs to be distilled for Usquebath.

Take Agrimony, Fumitory, Betony, Bugloss, Wormwood, Harts-tongue, Carduus Benedictus, Rosemary, Angelica, Tormentil, of each of these for every gallon of Ale one handful, Anniseed, and Liquorish well bruised half a pound, still these together, and when it is stilled, you must infuse Cinamon, Nutmeg, Mace, Liquorish, Dates, and Raisins of the Sun, and sugar what quantity you please. The infusion must be till the colour please you.

Dr. Kings way to make Mead.

Take five quarts and a pint of water, and warm it, then put one quart of Honey to every gallon of Liquor, one Lemon, and a quarter of an ounce of Nutmegs; it must boil till the scum rise black, that you will have it quickly ready to drink, squeeze into it a Lemon when you tun it. It must be cold before you tun it up.

To make Syrup of Rasberries.

Take nine quarts of Rasberries, clean pickt, and gathered in a dry day, and put to them four quarts of good Sack, into an earthen pot, then paste it up very close, and set it in a Cellar for ten days, then distill it in a Glass or Rosestill, then take more Sack and put in Rasberries to it, then when it hath taken out all the colour of the Raspis, strain it out and put in some fine Sugar to your taste, and set it on the fire, keeping it continually stirring till the scum doth rise; then take it off the fire, let it not boil, skim it very clean, and when it is cold put it to your distilled Raspis; colour it no more than to make it a pale Claret Wine. This put into bottles or Glasses stopt very close.

To make Lemon Water.

Take twelve of the fairest Lemons, slice them, and put them into two pints of White wine, and put to them Cinamon two drams, Gallingale two drams, of Rose-leaves, Borage and Bugloss flowers, of each one handful, of yellow Saunders one dram; steep all these together twelve hours; then distill them gently in a Glass still untill you have distilled one pint and an half of the Water, and then adde to it three ounces of Sugar; one grain of Ambergreese, and you will have a most pleasing cleansing Cordial water for many uses.

To make Gilly-flower Wine.

Take two ounces of dryed Gilly-flowers, and put them into a pottle of Sack, and beat three ounces of Sugar-candy, or fine Sugar and grind some Ambergreese, and put it in the bottle and shake it oft, then run it through a gelly bag, and give it for a great Cordial after a weeks standing or more. You may make Lavander as you do this.

The Lady Spotswood Stomach Water.

Take white Wine one pottle, Rosemary and Cowslip flowers, of each one handful, as much Betony leaves, Cinamon and Cloves grosly beaten, of both one ounce; steep all these three dayes, stirring it often; then put to it Mithridate four ounces, and stir it together, and distil it in an ordinary still.

Water of Time for the Passion of the Heart.

Take a quart of white Wine, and a pint of Sack, steep in it as much broad Thime as it will wet, put to it of Galingale and Calamus Aromaticus, of each one ounce, Cloves, Mace, Ginger, and grains of Paradise two drams, steep these all night, the next morning distil it in an ordinary still, drink it warm with Sugar.

A Receipt to make damnable Hum.

Take Species de Gemmis, Aromaticum Rosatum, Diarrhodon Abbatis, Lætificans Galeni, of each four drams, Loaf-sugar beaten to powder half a pound, small *Aqua Vitæ* three Pints, strong Angelica water one pint; mix all these together, and when you have drunk it to the Dregs, you may fill it up again with the same quantity of water. The same powders will serve twice, and after twice using it, it must be made new again.

An admirable Water for sore Eyes.

Take *Lapis Tutiæ*; Aloes Hepatica, fine hard sugar, of each three drams, beat them very small, and put them into a Glass of three pints, to which put red Rose-water and white Wine, of each one pint; set the Glass in the Sun, in the Month of *July*, for the whole Month, shaking it twice in a day for all that while; then use it as followeth, put one drop thereof into the Eye in the evening, when the party is in bed, and one drop in the morning an hour before the Patient riseth: Continue the use of it till the Eyes be well. The older the Water, the better it is. Most approved.

A Snail Water for weak Children, and old People.

Take a pottle of Snails, and wash them well in two or three waters, and then in small Beer, bruise them shells and all, then put them into a gallon of red Cows Milk, red Rose leaves dried, the whites cut off, Rosemary, sweet Marjoram, of each one handful, and so distil them in a cold still, and let it drop upon powder of white Sugar candy in the receiver; drink of it first and last, and at four a clock in the afternoon, a wine-glass full at a time.

Clary Water for the Back, Stomach, &c.

Take three gallons of midling Beer, put in a great brass Pot of four gallons, and put to it ten handfuls of Clary gathered in a dry day, Raisins of the Sun stoned three pounds, Anniseeds, and Liquorish, of each four ounces, the whites and shells of twenty four eggs, or half so many, if there be not so much need, beat the shells small, and mix them with the whites; put to the bottoms of three white loaves, put into the Receiver one pound of white sugar-candy, or so much fine loaf sugar beaten small, and distill it through a Limbeck, keep it close, and be seldom without it; for it reviveth very much the stomach and heart, strengtheneth the back, procureth appetite and digestion, driveth away Melancholly, sadness and heaviness of the heart, &c.

Dr. Montfords *Cordial Water.*

Take Angelica leaves twelve handfuls, six leaves of Carduus Benedictus, Balm & Sage, of each five handfuls, the seeds of Angelica and sweet Fennil, of each five ounces bruised, scraped and bruised Liquorish twelve ounces, Aromaticum Rosatum, Diamoscus dulcis, of each six drams; the Herbs being cut small, the seeds and Liquorish bruised, infuse them into two gallons of Canary Sack for twenty four hours, then distill it with a gentle fire, and draw off onely five pints of the spirits, which mix with one pound of the best Sugar dissolved into a Syrup in half a pint of pure red Rose-water.

Aqua Mirabilis, Sir Kenelm Digby's *way.*

Take Cubebs, Gallingale, Cardamus, Melliot flowers, Cloves, Mace, Ginger, Cinamon, of each one dram bruised small, juyce of Celandine one pint, juyce of Spearmint half a pint, juyce of Balm half a pint, sugar one pound, flower of Cowslips, Rosemary, Borage, Bugloss, Marigolds, of each two drams, the best Sack three pints, strong Angelica water one pint, red Rose-water half a pint, bruise the Spices and flowers, & steep them in the Sack & Juyces one night, the next morning distill it in an ordinary Limbeck or glass still, and first lay Hearts-tongue leaves in the bottom of the Still.

The Vertues of the precedent Water.

This Water preserveth the Lungs without grievances, and helpeth them; being wounded, it suffereth the blood not to putrifie, but multiplieth the same; this water suffereth not the heart to burn, nor melancholly, nor the Spleen to be lifted up above nature; it expelleth the Rheum, preserveth the Stomach, conserveth Youth, and procureth a good colour, it preserveth Memory, it destroyeth the palsie; if this be given to one a dying, a spoonful of it reviveth him; in the summer use one spoonful a week fasting, in the winter two spoonfuls.

A Water for fainting of the Heart.

Take Bugloss and red Rose-water of each one pint, Milk half a pint, Anniseeds and Cinamon grosly bruised, of each half an ounce, Maiden-hair two handfuls, Harts-tongue one handful, both shred, mix all together, and distill it in an ordinary still, drink of it morning and evening With a little sugar.

A Surfeit Water.

Take half a bushel of red Corn Poppy, put it into a large dish, cover it with brown Paper, and lay another dish upon it, set it in an Oven after brown bread is baked divers times till it be dry, which put into a pottle of good *Aqua vitæ*, to which put Raisins of the sun stoned half a pound, six figs sliced, three Nutmegs sliced, two flakes of Mace bruised, two races of Ginger sliced, one stick of Cinnamon bruised, Liquorish sliced one ounce, Aniseed, Fennil-seed, and Cardamums bruised, of each one dram; put all these into a broad glass body, and lay first some Poppy in the bottom, then some of the other ingredients, then Poppy again, and so untill the Glass be full; then put in the *Aqua vitæ*, and let it infuse till it be strong of the spices, and very red with the Poppy, close covered, of which take two or three spoonfuls upon a surfeit, and when all the liquor is spent, put more *Aqua vitæ* to it, and it will have the same effect the second time, but no more after.

Dr. Butlers *Cordial Water against Melancholly, &c. most approved.*

Take the flowers of Cowslips, Marigolds, Pinks, Clove-gilly-flowers, single stock gilly-flowers, of each four handfuls, the flowers of Rosemary, and Damask Roses, of each three handfuls, Borage and Bugloss flowers, and Balm leaves, of each two handfuls; put them in a quart of Canary Wine into a great Bottle or Jug close stopped, with a Cork, sometimes stirring the flowers and wine together, adding to them Anniseeds bruised one dram, two Nutmegs sliced, *English* Saffron two pennyworth; after some time of infusion, distill them in a cold Still with a hot fire, hanging at the Nose of the Still Ambergreece and Musk, of each one grain; then to the distilled water put White Sugar-candy finely beaten six ounces, and put the glass wherein they are into hot water for one hour. Take of this water at one time three spoonfuls thrice a week, or when you are ill, it cureth all melancholly fumes, and infinitely comforts the spirits.

The admirable and most famous Snail Water.

Take a peck of garden shell snails, wash them well in small beer, and put them in a hot Oven till they have done making a noise, then take them out, and wipe them well from the green froth that is upon them, and bruise them shells and all in a stone Mortar, then take a quart of earth worms, scower them with salt, slit them & wash them well with water from their filth, and in a stone Mortar beat them to pieces, then lay in the bottom of your distilled pot Angelica two handfuls, and two handfuls of Celandine upon them, to which put two quarts of Rosemary flowers, Bears foot, Agrimony, red Dock Roots, Bark of Barberries, Betony, Wood sorrel, of each two handfuls, Rue one handful; then lay the Snails and worms on the top of the Herbs and Flowers, then pour on three Gallons of the strongest Ale, and let it stand all night, in the morning put in three ounces of Cloves beaten, six penniworth of beaten Saffron and on the top of them six ounces of shaved Harts-horn, then set on the Limbeck, and close it with paste, and so receive the water by pints, which will be nine in all, the first is the strongest, whereof take in the morning two spoonfuls in four spoonfuls of small Beer, and the like in the afternoon; you must keep a good Diet and use moderate exercise to warm the blood.

This Water is good against all Obstructions whatsoever. It cureth a Consumption and Dropsie, the stopping of the Stomach and Liver. It may be distilled with milk for weak people and children, with Harts-tongue and Elecampance.

A singular Mint water.

Take a still full of Mints, put Balm, and Penniroyal, of each one good handful, steep them in Sack, or Lees of Sack twenty four hours, stop it close, and stir it now and then: Distill it in an ordinary Still with a very quick fire, and keep the Still with wet cloaths, put into the receiver as much sugar as will sweeten it, and so double distill it.

Distillings.

A most Excellent Aqua Coelestis taught by Mr. Philips Apothecary.

Take of Cinamon one dram, Ginger half a dram, the three sorts of Saunders, of each of them three quarters of an ounce, Mace and cubebs, of each of them one dram, Cardamom the bigger and lesser, of each three drams, Setwall-roots half an ounce, Anniseed, Fennil-seed Basil-seed, of each two drams, Angelica roots, Gilly-flowers, Thyme, Calamint, Liquorish, Calamus, Masterwort, Pennyroyal, Mint, Mother of Thyme, Marjoram, of each two drams, red Rose-seed, the flowers of Sage and Betony, of each a dram and a half, Cloves, Galingal, Nutmegs, of each two drams, the flowers of Stechados, Rosemary, Borage and Bugloss flowers, of each a dram and half, Citron Rindes three drams; bruise them all, and put in these Cordial Powders, Diamber Aromaticum, Diamascum, Diachoden, the Spices made with Pearl, of each three drams; infuse all these in twelve pints of *Aqua Vitæ*; in a glass, close stopped for fifteen dayes, often shaking it, then let it be put into a Limbeck close stopped, and let it be distilled gently; when you have done, hang in a cloth, two drams of Musk, half a dram of Ambergreese, and ten or twelve grains of gold, and so receive it to your use.

Hypocras taught by Dr. Twine for Wind in the Stomach.

Take Pepper, Grains, Ginger, of each half an ounce, Cinnamon, Cloves, Nutmegs, Mace, of each one ounce grosly beaten, Rosemary, Agrimony, both shred of each a few crops, red Rose leaves a pretty quantity, as an indifferent gripe, a pound of Sugar beaten; lay these to steep in a gallon of good Rhenish or white-Wine in a close vessel, stirring it two or three times a day the space of three or four dayes together, then strain it through an Hypocras strainer, and drink a draught of it before meat half an hour, and sometimes after to help digestion.

Marigold flowers distilled, good for the pain of the Head.

Take Marigold flowers, and distill them, then take a fine cloth and wet in the aforesaid distilled water, and so lay it to the forehead of the Patient, and being so applied, let him sleep if he can; this with Gods help will cease the pain.

A Water good for Sun burning.

Take Water drawn off the Vine dropping, the flowers of white Thorn, Bean-flowers, Water Lilly-flowers, Garden Lilly-flowers, Elder-flowers, and Tansie-flowers, Althea-flowers, the whites of Eggs, French Barley.

The Lady Giffords cordial Water.

Take four quarts of *Aqua vitæ*, Borrage and Poppy-water, of each a pint, two pounds of Sugar-candy, one pound of figs sliced, one pound of Raisins of the Sun stoned, two handfuls of red Roses clipped and dried, one handful of red Mint, half a handful of Rosemary, as much of Hysop, a few Cloves; put all these in a great double Glass close stopped, and set it in the sun three months, and so use it.

A water for one pensive and very sick, to comfort the Heart very excellent.

Take a good spoonful of *Manus Christi*, beaten very small into powder, then take a quarter of a pound of very fine sugar, and beat it small, and six spoonfuls of Cinamon water, and put to it, and ten spoonfuls of red Rose-water; mingle all these together, and put them in a dish, and set them over a soft fire five or six walms, and so let it be put into a glass, and let the party drink thereof a spoonful or two, as he shall see cause.

To perfume Water.

Take Malmsey or any kind of sweet water; then take Lavender, Spike, sweet Marjoram, Balm, Orange peels, Thyme, Basil, Cloves, Bay leaves, Woodbine flowers, red and white Roses, and still them all together.

FINIS.

Printed by BoD"in Norderstedt, Germany

9 781805 475262

BRISTOL SEAPORT

a pictorial history from the 1950s to the present day

COLIN MOMBER

redcliffe

First published in 1997 by Redcliffe Press, Bristol and Tiverton

Dedicated to Teresa, Mum and Dad and grandparents for whom the Bristol Docks were a way of life – and to Olive Crouch MBE and Reg Porter for their kindness to a young photographer in the 1960s.

British Library Cataloguing in Publication Data
A CIP catalogue record for this book is available from The British Library

ISBN 1 900178 70 2

REDCLIFFE PRESS
Halsgrove House
Lower Moor Way
Tiverton EX16 6SS
Tele: 01884 243242
Fax: 01884 243325

Printed and bound in Great Britain by Longdunn Press Ltd., Bristol

Contents

Introduction   4

Introduction to a Seaport: the City Docks   7

Avonmouth Dock   47

Portishead Dock   61

The Royal Edward Dock   69

Royal Portbury Dock   129

The Bristol Port Company: the Docks since 1991   149

Port-pourri   161

Index of Ships   176

Introduction

Ships and the bustle of waterfront life – for centuries the very essence of Bristol's being – have long vanished from the ancient harbour and winding wharves of the City Docks in the centre of the city. But the Port of Bristol is still very much alive, in good shape and on course for a smooth voyage to a long and prosperous future.

Today, the port no longer visually and economically dominates the life of the city as it did for many centuries when Bristol's success was almost totally linked to its maritime trading. The two major dock systems, sitting on opposite sides of the Avon's mouth, do however contribute substantially to the region's economy – and help retain Bristol's historic role as gateway to the west.

This illustrated book chronicles almost half-a-century of port life from the 1950s, when the last surviving steamships enhanced the docks with their majestic lines and graceful presence. By 1959, most ocean steamers were consuming their final bunkers of coal as they steamed into the sunset, leaving the high seas to the less glamorous but more efficient motor vessels. The era of modern shipping was sailing into the Sixties ...

The prosperous 1960s witnessed much port modernisation and, by the middle of the decade, there were more than 1800 ship movements a year, with imports and exports totalling almost nine million tons. Bristol had 40 import liner services covering almost every coastline in the world, as well as many short sea trades between the City Docks and Europe.

In September, 1967, decasualisation offered security of employment and fringe benefits not previously enjoyed by the port's 2000 dockers. This act of improved labour relations confined to history the archaic method of obtaining work by the waving of black books at prospective employers in the pens located in Prince Street and at Avonmouth.

The 1970s – a decade which was to see some of the most eventful years in port history – started as it would continue. On 26 October, 1970 came shock news: the Port Authority was £366,504 in the red – the first deficit in over thirty years. It was hard to believe. The quays, after all, were usually fully occupied and ships frequently double-berthed. But worse was to come. 1972 opened with a trio of disappointments: *Tideway*, the popular house magazine was axed; the port helicopter, a prestigious symbol of achievement, was sold off and, most devastating, Bristol City Line, after ninety-three years of continuous service between Bristol and New York, ceased trading, sold their ships and surrendered their proud name to Bibby Line.

By 1974, many of the great British shipping lines had disappeared or were in the process of reducing their fleets. It was a period of great change in trading patterns. Great Britain decided to join the European Community, in the process placing west coast ports at a disadvantage. By the mid-1970s, the golden years were over.

The unthinkable now happened. The City Docks, ancient harbour for over one thousand years, was closed to commercial shipping. For many of us, this was the unkindest cut of all.

At the decade's end, dozens of shipping companies had either merged or carried their final cargoes. The frozen meat trade was lost to containerisation and the mighty grain trade was hanging on by a husk. The port's extensive rail system was abandoned in favour of road transportation and its tracks torn up. The lock-gates of Avonmouth Old Dock were shut and sealed from the outside sea, just three months short of its centenary – scuppering, at the same time, any opportunity to celebrate the occasion.

So did anything positive happen during the 1970s?   Yes, the Royal Portbury Dock opened in 1977 – a dock designed to safeguard our future.   Its cost, though, imposed a crippling burden on an already struggling port and Bristol ratepayers had to foot the bill.   The tide was beginning to flow faster against Bristol, but contrary to the most gloomy predictions, it managed to avoid drowning during the decade that followed.

Bristol was not the only port in trouble.   Glasgow and Manchester were major casualties, while London – in an effort to come to terms with a fast changing world – had been phasing out groups of docks since 1967 and, by 1981, all the inner London systems were closed.   Tilbury in Essex was where future investment would be directed.

During the early 1980s, fears that the Port of Bristol might have little or no future were expressed by observers and employees.   The accounts for 1980-81 revealed a deficit of £10.8 million, and the battle for survival intensified.   General Manager Stanley Turner outlined the problems in the port newspaper:

> The delay in obtaining Government approval for Royal Portbury Dock increased the cost of construction and we are paying much higher interest rates than ever we anticipated.   This has exhausted our reserves.   Only two of Portbury's six berths have been developed and even if these two work at full capacity they could never meet the capital repayment and interest charges.   Tonnage through Avonmouth Docks has been reduced more quickly than anticipated.   We now have too many people in virtually all departments of the port against the amount of traffic we handle.   To survive we must increase our income and reduce our expenditure.

The PBA wasn't about to throw in the towel.   A generous voluntary redundancy package was devised involving every section of the Bristol Docks undertaking.   Hundreds decided to accept, and start a new life elsewhere.   Many didn't wish to leave but felt it the only safe passage in which to travel.   The port, after all, was a most interesting place to work, particularly on the waterfront where a unique dockside vocabulary and camaraderie was shared by dockers.   Their special style of badinage and dockside drollery amid the comings and goings of ships was a way of life unlikely to be encountered elsewhere.

Despite a significant shedding of labour, the deficit continued to mount, with cargo handling barely exceeding three million tons a year.   When Stanley Turner retired in 1983, he was succeeded by Gordon Scott Morris who took on the new job title of Port Director.   It made little difference.   He, too, had to preside over ebbing morale and dwindling dues.   The port was on the ropes, but wasn't about to stop fighting ... not as long as there was water in the dock.

The second half of the 1980s brought fresh hope and renewed confidence.   A radical restructuring of the port's finances by the City Council reduced its debt to £3.9 million.   In a surprise move the Docks Committee promoted the port's chief electrical engineer, Nasim Ahmad, to the post of Port Director.   Nasim, known for his pragmatic approach to problems and, conscious of the trust placed in him, had no plans to go down with a sinking ship.   Further efficiency measures were implemented, at both quayside and managerial levels.   Very slowly the tide began to turn.

During 1989 the National Dock Labour Board was phased out and most of the dockers elected to leave the industry when a new redundancy deal was introduced.   New men were trained and office staff were frequently recruited to help discharge vessels at peak periods.   Labour became more fluid and the PBA could at last realise an ambition it had harboured for years – to offer a flexible service.   This was a positive change in the port's attitude and at dockside level it could be most keenly felt.

The trade year ending in March 1991 saw tonnages up to 4.7 million – the highest for sixteen years.   PBA superintendent Roger Pratt, praising the workforce, said: 'Cargoes are being discharged faster and more efficiently than ever before.   Port operatives have given an outstanding performance since November 1990.'

His terminology was significant – port operatives had replaced dockers.   The port was on the threshold of the biggest reshaping period since decasualisation nearly a quarter of a century earlier. That reshaping was about to reach proportions hitherto undreamed of in port thinking.

On 27 August, 1991, the biggest administrative upheaval since 1848 took place, marking in stone another date for the city's history books. The Port of Bristol Authority, lacking the investment needed to sustain long-term growth, handed the tiller to two businessmen – Terence Mordaunt and David Ord – in a deal worth £36 million pounds linked to a 150-year lease. With careful planning and hefty investment, this new Bristol Port Company has since transformed Bristol's docks into a vibrant and profitable workplace again. Another chapter has opened in the long history of Bristol Port, bringing in its wake optimism and the promise of a permanent return to the maritime greatness synonymous for so many centuries with the City and County of Bristol.

St Augustine's Reach, constructed between 1240-47 by diverting the course of the River Frome, now enjoys a more tranquil existence in the wake of seven and a half centuries of commercial activity.

Introduction to a Seaport: the City Docks

Where it all began ... Queen Square dominates this aerial view of central Bristol with the River Frome diversion, completed in 1247, clearly seen on the left.   The original course of the Avon can be see passing under Bristol bridge [middle top], Redcliffe bridge [right] and Prince Street bridge [bottom].

William Sloan's *Talisker*, 1016 tons, loads general cargo for Glasgow and Belfast at Cripp's Corner early in 1965. This modern motor coaster, along with the vessels *Fruin*, *Kelvin* and *Tay*, replaced a fleet of beautiful steamers which had been employed on this triangular coastal trade since the beginning of the century.

'In the middle of the street, as far as you can see, hundreds of ships, their masts as thick as they can stand by one another, which is the oddest and most surprising sight imaginable ...' So wrote poet Alexander Pope after a visit to Bristol in 1739.

The ships which plied the trade routes have changed out of all recognition but the unique atmosphere of this ancient harbour – with its backdrop of churches, inns, historic landmarks and cobbled hauling-ways – endured until the city docks were phased out in the 1970s. During this period the gradual demolition of cranes and other maritime trappings created acres of desolate wharfage and, at the same time, brought to an end a thousand years of water-borne trading in the very harbour which gave birth to Bristol and made it the largest commercial centre in the west country.

Exactly when the first settlers established a community at the confluence of the rivers Avon and Frome is not known.   But from the evidence of unearthed coins and artefacts, it is known that by 1000 AD Bristol housed a mint, was fortified and recognised as a bridge point with sea-trading links with South Wales and Ireland.

In 1239, work started on a massive scheme to extend the port.   Eight years later, and at a cost of £5000, a mighty trench 2000 feet long had been excavated from the top end of what is now known as the Centre through to the Arnolfini corner.   This diverted the flow of the Frome, which used to enter the Avon near Bristol Bridge after winding its way along what is now Baldwin Street. Navigational access was improved greatly, and the creation of the Broad and Narrow Quays provided increased wharf space for the discharge and loading of cargoes.   The separate parish of Redcliffe, on the Somerset side of the Avon, was asked to contribute to this major port improvement.

In 1373, Bristol was granted county status and independence from Gloucestershire.   During the fourteenth and fifteenth centuries its industrial output increased, with trade links extended to Iberia and Iceland.   In the wake of John Cabot's epic voyage to the North American mainland in 1497, entrepreneurial eyes were turned west-wards.   The Society of Merchant Venturers, founded in 1551, did much to promote trade with the New World and, eventually, with West Africa, the Caribbean, Mediterranean and the Baltic Seas.   It was the dawn of a golden era which would last for two centuries.   Its unrivalled geographical position, the establishment of the West Indian colonies and the far-reaching expertise of its maritime merchants had made Bristol the second port in the kingdom.

By the end of the eighteenth century, however, Bristol's importance started to slide.   With the major shortcoming of the enormous rise and fall of Avon's tide, which forced all vessels to be drydocked at their berths twice in the natural day – causing stress to hull and ship-owner alike – and the emergence of Liverpool as a major seafaring city, something drastic needed to be done.

The Merchant Venturers invited William Jessop to find ways to improve the harbour.   In August, 1802 his plan for a floating harbour was accepted and submitted to parliament for approval.   Work began in 1804 and was completed in April, 1809 at a cost of £600,000 – twice the original estimate. The Port of Bristol was transformed. An area of 89 acres of water had been impounded by locks constructed at Hotwells and Netham along with the excavation of a three-mile river diversion to allow the tidal Avon to flow around the dockised section.

Dependent on their dimensions, ships now had to enter harbour through one of two sets of locks.   The north lock measured 200 feet by 45 feet and the south entrance was 185 feet by 35 feet.   Both were inadequate within a few years. Vessels then sailed into a 700 feet by 300 feet holding basin, named after the Duke of Cumberland, before moving into the main dock area. At that time most facilities were still situated at Broad and Narrow Quays, the Grove, and the Redcliffe and Welsh Backs. The Bristol Dock Company was formed to operate the new undertaking but, because of the crippling cost of construction, could not afford to develop it properly. Attempts to remain solvent resulted in the charging of excessive port dues, and trade was driven to rival ports.

The Corporation assumed control of the docks in 1848, dues were reduced and the loss of trade was staunched. In 1873 new, enlarged locks 350 feet by 62 feet were opened at Cumberland Basin and during the next thirty years fine granite quays were constructed at Dean's Marsh, Canon's Marsh, and Prince's, Bathurst and Wapping Wharves. These new deep-water berths replaced the natural slopes of the river bank. Rail links were extended to serve seven new transit sheds.

Some ancient berths were sacrificed during this period of modernisation. Between 1895 and 1938 sections of the Frome were gradually covered over and lost from public view as increased road traffic necessitated the creation of the Tramway Centre, which is still the hub of Bristol's traffic system. The water was reduced to 82 acres, but with 4 miles of waterfront facilities the City Docks were well equipped to cater for the increasing trade which was due, in some measure, to an upsurge in industrial activity.

After the First World War, the rivermouth docks took care of most of the long-haul trade routes, with the floating harbour handling the European and coastal trade. This accounted for around one million tons of cargo a year – a notable contribution to the port's total turnover.

In January, 1970 came the unwelcome news that the City Docks were to be phased out and closed to commercial shipping. Hemmed into a mid-town location with no further hope of expansion, coupled with an increased contribution to road traffic congestion, they had become increasingly uneconomic to run. The motorways had arrived and more effective methods of transportation were being introduced on land and sea. There was no alternative but to bow to the inevitable.

Today, the harbour is given over largely to recreational pursuits. Rowing regattas, water festivals and open-air concerts all have a role to play, and waterside homes are bringing people back to live in the city. The former docks are now promoted as Bristol Historic Harbour and, with the promise of National Lottery funds, the area has a potentially very exciting future. There is no doubt, either, that the immensely successful Festival of the Sea in 1996 has done much to bring Bristol's attractions to a wider audience. But for the purist, there are far too few maritime focal points of interest. 'Messing about in boats' is no substitute for the real thing. With the notable exception of the s.s. *Great Britain*, the city has in the past missed the opportunity to secure some historically interesting vessels, including the beautiful steam tug *Bristolian* and the *Bristol Queen*, pride of the White Funnel fleet. There were others before them. Bristol needs to attract, and keep, more real ships if it is to retain at its heart any real flavour of its colourful maritime past.

More woodpulp for St Anne's Board Mills goes overside to Ashmead barges from the Norwegian vessel *Havpil*, 1037 tons, at L Shed, Prince's Wharf, in June 1969. Along the quay at M Shed is the Bristol ship *Dido*, 1589 tons, loading for Dublin.

Heavily laden, the thirty-five-year old veteran of many a North Sea crossing arrives at Hotwells in 1955 with woodpulp and heavy machinery. After discharge, this fine-looking ship steamed back to Sweden full of British machinery.

Almost home ... the m.v. *Pluto* rounds the final bend of the Avon after a winter voyage from Antwerp in 1955. This 988-ton vessel served the Bristol Steam Navigation Company for seventeen years before she was sold to an Italian company in 1967. She was lost in heavy seas off Malta in 1972.

Afternoon strollers gather around the Cumberland Basin locks to watch the 1920-built, 1476-ton Swedish steamer *Dagmar Bratt* come into port on a sunny Sunday in July 1955 – ten years before the new road system so dramatically transformed the landscape.   Ships of the Bratt Line were a familiar sight in the City Docks for many years.   On the right is the Dockmaster's house with its clocktower, and a group of lockgate-men, smartly dressed in their nautical gear, sadly rarely worn today.

Waiting for summertime ... during the winter months, paddle steamers of P. and A. Campbell's White Funnel Fleet moored up in some of the quieter reaches of the Floating Harbour.   One favourite spot was the Underfall Yard where, during November, 1955 the 765-ton *Cardiff Queen* was pictured along with two King's tugs, *Volunteer* and *John King*, waiting for the next high water.

The *Cardiff Queen*, one of six pleasure steamers in service that year, came to Bristol in June, 1947 and made her last commercial voyage with 400 passengers to Lundy Island on 21 September, 1966.   Companion ships in 1955 were: *Britannia*, *Ravenswood*, *Glen Usk*, *Glen Gower* and *Bristol Queen*.   These lovely white steamers gradually disappeared until on 31 August, 1967 the pride of the fleet – *Bristol Queen* – was taken out of service.   Many ardently hoped she would remain as a tourist attraction and maritime museum, but on 22 March, 1968 she made a final voyage from Cardiff to an Ostend breakers' yard.

C. J. King's tiniest tug, the 32-ton *Volunteer*, tows the 1922, Oslo-built steamer *Baltkon*, 1570 tons, into Cumberland Basin with a full cargo of esparto grass from North Africa, in summer, 1956. Esparto is used in the manufacture of high grade paper and bank notes, and was frequently shipped through the City Docks.

The two waterfront inns on the right, The Pilot and The Star, were demolished in the mid-1960s for the Plimsoll bridge improvement scheme. Cumberland Basin was named after the Duke of Cumberland who visited Bristol in 1803 to discuss defence plans against Napoleon.

Where Frome greets Avon ... a view from Prince's Wharf towards St Augustine's Reach on a summer evening in 1956. The heavy-lift steam crane to the left was removed in 1961 after a working life of sixty-eight years, although its stone-built base remains. To its rear is the William Sloan Line's T Shed, destroyed by fire in the 1970s and replaced by a car park. Jury's Hotel now stands across the Reach at Narrow Quay. And the ships – the saddest loss of all – have long gone.

Grand old lady of the high seas ... this 1751-ton steamer, built in 1920, had character and, along with the cobblestones, added atmosphere to the Narrow Quay at the Bush warehouse corner [now Arnolfini] when photographed in 1956.

A real eye-catcher at Baltic Wharf ... the bright red hull and cream superstructure of this 3325-ton Lauritzen liner turned many a head in October, 1956 when she arrived at Prince's Wharf from Finland with a cargo of plywood, newsprint and woodpulp.

This interesting 1230-ton Danish steamship, built in 1937, is berthed at Bathurst Basin Wharf in 1957. The old-style cranes were replaced by modern ones in the early-1960s, which were later transferred to Portishead. The John Robinson Oil Mill and the old Bathurst East and West transit sheds were eventually torn down to make way for waterfront houses and offices.

The 300-foot *Esbjorn Gorthon*, 1969 tons, at Canon's Marsh in 1955 dwarfs the 939-ton BSN vessel *Cato* lying astern. An unlucky ship, *Cato* ran down and sank the river tug *Sea Prince* in 1957 and, in May, 1963 was herself rammed and sunk in the Royal Edward Dock by the *City of Brooklyn*. Ahead of Ashmead's barge *Leander*, the old steam cranes can be seen at Wapping Wharf. Nine years later the wharf was modernised, and four lofty Blue Streaks stood in their stead.

Bristol Steam's *Milo*, 991 tons, was such a revolutionary design that she was put on show to the public at Broad Quay immediately after the builders, Charles Hill & Sons, handed her over to BSN in March, 1953. Used mainly on the Antwerp and Rotterdam run, she is pictured in the early-1960s making her way through the Floating Harbour to her A Shed berth at Canon's Marsh. HMS *Flying Fox* and pleasure steamer *Bristol Queen* are both moored at Mardyke Wharf to the left. Opposite, the Albion Dockyard cranes stand tall on the skyline.

Woodpulp, the principal commodity at the City Docks, was loaded into F. A. Ashmead's barges when the regular trader m.v. *Stanford*, 1523 tons, was at Prince's Wharf during the 1960s. Shifting barges alongside the Standard liner is the *Judith-A*, which had been converted from a steam tug to a motor tug – losing an attractive funnel in the process. This 1915-built craft, formerly named *Conroy*, had an eventful working life: in 1929, when Ashmeads acquired her, she proved to be the last vessel to navigate the entire length of the Kennet and Avon Canal from Reading to Bath before it silted up. She was eventually sold in the early-1980s and shipped out to West Africa aboard a Sif liner.

Sundown at the City Docks.

A good day's work ... F. A. Ashmead's barges, laden with woodpulp, moor at Bush's corner before being towed along the Feeder Canal to St Anne's Board Mills in summer, 1963.   Seven years later Ashmeads lost around 100,000 tons of barge trade when a new woodpulp terminal opened at Portishead.   Afterwards, only 12 barges in the Ashmead fleet were transferred to Avonmouth; the remainder, unsuitable for the Lydney log trade, were sold or broken up.

Busy corner ... all part of waterfront life in 1963 with the 1523-ton Norwegian pulp and timber carrier, *Stanford*, berthed at Narrow Quay on Bush's corner. Today, gazing across a harbour largely devoid of ships, a bronze representation of John Cabot sits here, surrounded by restaurant tables and seats.

The Russian training ship *Zenit*, 4374 tons, was the largest ship, by tonnage, ever to enter the City Docks, when she docked at M Shed on 21 May, 1963 with a cargo of plywood, beating the previous record holder, s.s. *Magunkook*, 4029 tons, which in August, 1919 brought in 4500 tons of meal from Savannah.

346 feet long, the *Zenit* was certainly not the longest vessel to negotiate the River Avon – that distinction belongs to the 358-foot French steamer *Fhrygie*, which came into the Floating Harbour during the First World War. And just ten months before the *Zenit*, the 356-foot *Heinrich Grammerstorf*, 3917 tons, docked at Prince's Wharf with a load of lumber from Leningrad.

Scandinavian pulpers...the Norwegian vessel, *Stanford*, 1523 tons, along with the Swedish *Gertrude Bratt*, 1530 tons, occupy around 600 feet of the Narrow Quay for the discharge of woodpulp to barge and shore during the mid-1960s. Dominating the background is the old CWS building, demolished in 1974, while construction of the new Unicorn Hotel is well under way. This ancient quay is today lined with trees and provides a pleasant recreational walkway together with ample mooring for a variety of pleasure boats.

Quiet backwater ... Bathurst Basin was created when the Floating Harbour was built during 1803-09, offering shipping, via the New Cut, an alternative entrance into the upper reaches of the City Docks. With the lock measuring only 155 feet by 36 feet it surely was unlikely that vessels exceeding 500 tons gross would have entered. In 1935 the navigational rights were phased out and, by 1951, the lock entrance was sealed with a concrete dam.

Ten years later, when this picture was taken, Bathurst Basin was one of the few quiet havens where private boats could be moored safely away from the shipping lanes. Major improvements in the 1980s provided extended small boat facilities, landscaping and waterfront homes which replaced the storage sheds.

The early-1960s: cobblestones, handcarts, barges loaded with woodpulp, the once familiar BSN building in Wapping Road, and the stern of Brass T liner, *Becky*, at Prince's Wharf.   All that survives today is the cobbled quay outside Arnolfini.

Nothing stirs ... a quiet Sunday afternoon at the City Docks in 1965 with Dutch coasters *Grebbestrom*, 748 tons, and the 396-ton *Zaanborg*, berthed at Dean's Marsh. The Brass T Swedish *Irene*, 1559 tons, along with m.v. *Pluto*, 988 tons, are in the distance at Prince's Wharf.   Ashmead barges lie empty at Narrow Quay waiting for Monday morning, when hatch covers will open, cranes start nodding and cargoes get moving.

The sleek little pleasure craft *Lady Betty* passes gracefully between the General Steam Navigation's *Woodlark*, 933 tons, at Dean's Marsh, and the Transmarin liner, *Irene*, 1559 tons, at Prince's Wharf, one summer evening in 1965.

The Redcliffe bascule bridge opens to allow a Bristol Sand and Gravel dredger through as it leaves the Redcliffe Wharf for the Bristol Channel to dredge for sand in the mid-1960s. Built at the Albion Dockyard in 1956, the 610-ton *Badminton* has another three bridges to negotiate, locks to pass through and a 6-mile river voyage before reaching the open sea. The bascule bridge, built in 1942, is rarely raised today.

The 979-ton William Sloan coaster *Kelvin*, pictured at Cripp's corner in 1966, along with the bow of BSN's m.v. *Pluto*, was another of the motor vessels which replaced the old, but more eye-catching, steamers such as *Findhorn*, *Brora* and *Beauly*.   The line was taken over by Coast Lines in 1958, but the Sloan name and livery remained until 30 April, 1968.   Then, beaten by drive-on ferries and containerisation, the last of the Scotchers, the m.v. *Tay*, left Bristol for Belfast on a final voyage ... so ending 110 years of trade between England, Ireland and Scotland.

Well-known Holms Sand and Gravel dredger *Steep Holm*, 532 tons, is seen discharging sand at The Grove in the mid-1960s.   Built in Bristol in 1950, she was wrecked after going aground on Tusker Rock, near Porthcawl, on 2 October, 1968.

Heading for town ... a new weekly service was introduced by Gotha Line on 26 February, 1968 between the City Docks and Sweden, replacing the service previously operated by the Bratt Line. The m.v. *Fraternia*, 498 tons, one of two vessels employed on this run, moves into Sea Mills Reach *en route* for T Shed at Dean's Marsh, the old William Sloan berth. Cargo was discharged through a side port by forklift trucks.

Pleasure craft *Lady Betty* speeds by as a shipment of coke is loaded to coaster at the Canon's Marsh Works on 12 April, 1968. Over 17,000 tons of coke were exported from this berth every year.

Timber ... and plenty of it aboard this Russian 3000-tonner, which arrived at Cumberland Basin in 1968, with a deck-high parcel of lumber all the way from Igarka, 200 miles up the Yenisei river in Siberia.

With the City Docks handling around one million tons of general cargo every year throughout the 1960s, river traffic was part of the Bristol scene.   Visitors like this Russian timber carrier, under tow in 1967, did much to enhance the beauty of the Avon Gorge.

Sunday strollers pass along Prince's Wharf during April, 1969 while the side-loader *Fraternia*, 498 tons, Dutch coaster *Arrow*, 500 tons, and the 1139-ton *Charente* idle away time until the Monday morning workforce arrive.

Round the bend ... Bristol Steam Navigation liner *Hero*, 1580 tons, is Dublin-bound and deck-high with Bristol goods as she takes the Horseshoe Bend in July, 1968.

The m.v. *Dido* approaches the City Docks after an eighteen-hour voyage from Dublin on 6 August, 1968. Originally designed for the steel trade from South Wales to the Continent, she entered service in October, 1963, the last vessel built for the Bristol Steam Navigation Company. Like her sister *Hero*, she proved unsuitable for conversion to container work and was sold in November, 1969.

Trade route ... the River Avon, Bristol's most vital artery for a thousand years, on 28 October, 1968: the outward-bound, 322 feet-long Russian steamer *Verkhoyansk*, 2950 tons, is being towed to the open sea by C. J. King's tug *Sea Alert*. Heading for the City Docks, with a line of barges under tow, is the Port Authority tug *Cabot*.

The submarine *Alaric* gets a fast tow to Narrow Quay by the river tug *John King* in December, 1968 when she and HMS *Sealion* paid a courtesy visit to the City Docks.

Tight squeeze ... with a gap of only one foot either side, the m.v. *Charente*, 1139 tons, eases her 40-foot beam through the 42-foot junction cut at Prince Street bridge in October, 1969.

These attractive cranes at W and E Sheds, at the City Centre, were installed in 1894 and powered by dock water pumped through a pipe at 750 pounds per square inch from a hydraulic power station at Underfall Yard – over a mile away.   On this day, 9 December, 1969, there were 143 cranes of different designs and lifting capacities throughout the Port of Bristol.   These little beauties, modernised in the 1960s, were still the fastest cargo-shifters in the business until they were scrapped in 1970.

Sherry galore ... over 900 barrels of Harveys sherry were unloaded from the 500-ton Dutch coaster *Imke* on 9 December, 1969, by the fast-moving hydraulic cranes at W Shed.   The CWS building, on the right, was demolished in the summer of 1974.

Passing Round Point and steering a course for Wapping Wharf is this lumber-laden Russian ship in October, 1969.

Renwick out – Russian in ... river traffic meet up between Black Rock and Round Point during the autumn of 1969.

The 1145-ton *Stena Paper* is berthed at F Site with a cargo of forest produce from Sweden, while cases of tobacco, up river from Avonmouth, are discharged from the Benjamin Perry barge *Rhodesia* at the historic Mud Dock near the Prince Street bridge during October, 1969.

The waters of the Avon and Severn are heavily charged with mud.   Constant dredging within the enclosed docks is vital to maintain deep-water berths and shipping channels.   The 1963 *BD7*, now employed along the Feeder Canal, was pictured in 1969 making a contribution to Port cleanliness by loading 60 tons of silt from the dock floor into the hold of the motor hopper *Kenn*, near Prince Street bridge.

Behind, at Bathurst Wharf, regular Norwegian visitor, the 1426-ton *Biscaya* discharged a much cleaner cargo of woodpulp to barges and lorries.

Time to let go ... as they passed the maritime village of Pill, the river tug *John King* released the towing rope and allowed the 3952-ton Transmarine liner *Neva* a clear passage to the open sea as she returned to Sweden in May, 1970.

The City Docks enjoyed a unique atmosphere, quite different to the modern ocean docks at the rivermouth. Here, during August 1970, the 3860-ton *Inga*, at Wapping Wharf, discharges woodpulp from Husum in northern Germany, while the MacAndrews fruit carrier *Churnuca*, 1577 tons, is berthed at A Shed, with a shipload of goods from Spain.

The most modern of the City Docks' cranes are seen working at A Shed and Wapping Wharf in 1968. The Blue Streaks, discharging wood-pulp from the m.v. *Gloria*, jib easily across the ship as they transfer the pulp to barge.

33

Last hurrahs ... Leyland car parts being loaded to the 500-ton Dutch coaster *Emmy S* at Prince's Wharf, one of ten ships working in the City Docks on 27 August, 1970.   This was the last busy spell for the historic harbour – within three years the cranes were toppled, and the berths empty ... henceforth, trading would be confined to the rivermouth docks.

Short-term investment ... within a few years of modernising Wapping Wharf to accommodate larger ships and their timber cargoes from Scandinavia and Russia, the City Council steered the City Docks on a closure course – which came all too quickly.

Double Dutch ... Rotterdam coasters *Oosterburgh* and *Marinus Smits*, both 499 tons gross, were neighbours for a day on 27 August, 1970 – time enough to off-load their cargoes and take time out for a little painting.

Funnel of distinction ... Scandinavian lumber is off-loaded from this lovely old Norwegian freighter, the s.s. *Vard*, 1938 tons, which spent a week at Wapping Wharf during August, 1970.

Down she goes ... a sad moment in March, 1971 as this crane – the last of three at F Site – crashes down on the quay.   Within two years all but five of the Floating Harbour's 42 cranes had been dismantled or destroyed – changing irrevocably a unique city skyline.

Last of the line ... Captain Fred Hobart, Dock Master at the City Docks, pictured on duty at Wapping Wharf during November, 1971: he was the last of a long line of Dock Masters in command of the shipping movements in and out of the ancient harbour. When Fred retired in 1976, the transformation from commercial to recreational use was well under way – the only regular traders now were the sand dredgers.   With the changing pattern of dock life, a new, all-embracing post was created – that of Harbour Master.

Now a parking lot, F Site alongside the Grove once enjoyed the happier atmosphere of dockers working the many timber ships which berthed there until it closed in March, 1971.

Stout shipment ... a familiar site at M Shed was the importation of giant casks of Guinness – a cargo which helped the Bristol Steam Navigation Company remain in the black until September, 1971. Guinness then decided to divert these liquid assets through Liverpool, thus terminating a 145-year drinks link with the Port of Bristol.

Children at Sea Mills Reach watch the m.v. *Konstantin Savillev*, 1813 tons, head for the open sea after discharging her cargo of timber at Wapping Wharf in September, 1972. Watching ships run the river was a pleasure soon to be denied Bristolians, as the gradual closure of the City Docks in the early 1970s meant fewer and fewer vessels navigating the scenic 6 miles between Hotwells and Avonmouth.

All gone ... not a trace remains of these timber drying sheds, pictured in 1972, at the Hotwells end of Spike Island.   The area is now covered with waterside homes.

Away she goes!   A launching was always an event at the Charles Hill Albion Dockyard, with traffic stopping and people gathering across the water at Hotwell Road, watching and wondering if the new vessel would stop short of the Mardyke Wharf as its stern came rapidly towards them.   Most did – and this 733-ton oil rig was no exception as she hurtled down the slipway in 1973.

'Goodbye, old girl, we'll miss you' – sentiments shared by the sea cadets of t.s. *Adventure* and Bristolians as HMS *Flying Fox* leaves the City Docks on her final voyage to a Cardiff breakers' yard on Sunday evening, 18 March, 1973. Crowds lined the Cumberland Basin for a final look, and the sea cadets piped farewell as she was towed through the locks into the Avon – the river she last saw in 1923, when she first steamed into port. Built at Wallsend-on-Tyne in 1916, this 276-foot-long RNVR ship had been a feature of the Hotwells waterfront for fifty years. Mardyke Wharf still looks naked without her.

The 260-foot gridiron, built in 1884 just outside Cumberland Basin, allows ships to drydock themselves for a few hours between high water for hull inspection or minor repairs. Occupying this temporary dry spot in the winter of 1973 was this Newport-registered coaster of 490 tons.

Holms sand dredger *Harry Brown*, 634 tons, tries to steer a course through a dock full of sail boats to her berth at The Grove during the Water Festival in June, 1974.   HMS *Hecate* was open to the public at L Shed.

Speed and grace ... by 1975, when this picture was taken, speedboat racing had become a popular annual event in the harbour, while the s.s. *Great Britain* was gradually regaining her former grandeur after five years in the Wapping Dry Dock.   In 1970, optimists claimed that within two years the stately steamer would be fully restored.   Continuing restoration work is now well into its third decade.

Summer visitor ... HMS *Hecate* berthed at the Narrow Quay during a courtesy visit in 1976. One of 13 Royal Navy survey vessels, she occasionally carried out ice patrols in the South Atlantic.

Two ships undergoing repairs fit easily into the 542-foot long Albion Dry Dock during 1977. Since then few vessels have made use of this valuable facility which, in common with the Royal Edward Dry Dock at Avonmouth, has remained unused for several years.

A pair of Plimsolls – the bust of Samuel Plimsoll looks towards the sea as the 394-ton bucket dredger *Samuel Plimsoll* makes her final voyage from the City Docks in May, 1977.   The bust of Samuel Plimsoll, who was born at 9 Colston Parade, Redcliffe in 1824, was unveiled on 24 July, 1962 by the Lord Mayor of Bristol, Ald. L. Stevenson after being presented to the Docks Committee by the City Museum.   The site, at the entrance to the Floating Harbour, was chosen so that those afloat might see the man, and those ashore might see his mark on the ships that pass by.   The mud dredger was then moored at Avonmouth until she eventually departed from the port in which she was built in 1956 to start a new life dredging in Palermo, Sicily.

Taking the waters at Hotwells ... the Floating Harbour became a playground for water sports enthusiasts in the 1970s as commercial shipping was gradually eased out. These skiers were passing one of the few ships still using the dock in 1977, the 748-ton sand dredger *Peterston*.

Survey vessel HMS *Hecla* clears the Cumberland Basin locks on 30 September, 1982 after a courtesy visit to the City Docks.   The port's three tobacco bonds dominate the scene.

The largest vessel to navigate St Augustine's Reach for many years berthed at U Shed, Dean's Marsh, during April, 1983. The Singapore-registered *Logos*, 2319 tons, brought a cargo of educational and Christian literature, along with messages of hope and international fellowship. Owned by a British charity, Educational Book Exhibits, she visited 103 countries in her seventeen years on the high seas, spreading goodwill until she was shipwrecked near the southern tip of South America in January, 1988. Her replacement, *Logos 2*, was put in service in 1990 and visited Avonmouth Old Dock that September.

Totterdown Lock – or what little remains of it – was one of four original entrances into the City Docks. It led from the New Cut near Temple Meads directly into Totterdown Basin but, with the modest dimensions of 100 feet by 18 $\frac{1}{2}$ feet, it was suitable only for barges and small craft. It was land-filled during the Second World War lest a direct hit released the waters of the Floating Harbour. Today, much of it lies concealed beneath the busy Cattle Market Road.

Avonmouth Dock

Cory's tug *Pengarth* tows the sleek *Hardwicke Grange*, 9234 tons, alongside the repair jetty at the Old Dock during the spring of 1977.

[overleaf] Port prosperity ... well, it certainly appeared so when this photograph of Avonmouth Old Dock was taken in May 1972.   The locks were aimed at the open sea and all available land was in use with an extensive rail system surrounding the 21-acre dock.   Hard to believe that, within a decade, the change in trading patterns would see this dock end up losing most of its established tenants.   It looks an entirely different place in the 1990s.

There was no royal presence at the cutting of the first sod on 26 August, 1868 when work started on the construction of Avonmouth Dock; nor was there at the grand opening ceremony on 24 February, 1877, when the Mayor of Bristol declared it 'open to the commerce of the whole world'.

There was, however, much jubilation by the citizens of Bristol – and rightly so, for these dates not only signalled the beginning of what would become Bristol's greatest industrial suburb but were ultimately responsible for the city's western expansion in the early 1900s and helped Bristol retain its status as one of the major seaports in the United Kingdom.

Following the construction of the s.s. *Great Britain* in 1843, the size of ships began to increase, bringing into question the City Docks' ability to take these larger vessels. There were, in the 1850s, men of bold spirits and clear vision who recognised the need for deep water expansion if Bristol was to keep pace with the prosperity of rival ports – not at the City Docks but at the mouth of the Avon. Controversy raged: merchants whose interests were linked with the old docks resisted any rivermouth proposals; while city councillors couldn't agree upon the worthiness of constructing a new dock. Others, while acknowledging the advantages of a new ocean dock, could not decide as to which side of the river to construct it.

The Port and Pier Railway, which provided a link between Hotwells and the marshlands of Avonmouth, created the impetus to galvanise the men of more enlarged ideas into action when it opened to passenger traffic on 6 March, 1865. The Corporation declined to get involved, so the Bristol Port Channel Dock Company was formed under the chairmanship of Mr P. Miles of Kingsweston House, who owned the land on which the new dock was to be developed.

The ground-breaking ceremony actually took place on 26 August, 1868, and there followed over eight years of pick and shovel toil to dig the hole and erect the quays and shore facilities at a cost of £383,000. Serious delays occurred when large sections of quayage collapsed and had to be rebuilt.

Eventually the big day arrived and the mayor, Alderman George Edwards, along with 450 selected guests, locked out of Cumberland Basin on 24 February, 1877 aboard Bristol Steam Navigation's paddle steamer *Juno* bound for the new 16-acre enterprise 6 miles downstream. Hundreds of spectators cheered amid a profusion of flags and bunting as the *Juno* steamed into the 454 feet by 70 feet lock, which was 104 feet longer than the locks at Cumberland Basin. Using the paddlebox as a platform, the mayor declared the dock open. Facing a sea of bowed heads, the Archdeacon of Bristol then offered prayers for divine guidance in all its undertakings.

The *Juno*, cutting the ceremonial ribbon as she did, steamed into the dock, which measured 1400 feet by 500 feet, past the four newly-constructed transit sheds, came about, back through the locks to steer a course for the City Docks with all haste as the tide was by then ebbing.

The first vessel to trade at Avonmouth Dock was the s.s. *Evelyn*, which arrived on 8 April, 1877 with a cargo of barley from Sulina on the River Danube. Having a dock within Bristol waters operating in competition with the City Docks was, however, in the interests of very few people and, in September 1884, the City purchased the dock and, under the control of the Port of Bristol Authority, a more secure future was assured.

In 1895, an extension arm, 800 feet by 180 feet, to the south-west corner created another four acres of shipping space. Later, a section of the Junction Cut, which was to connect the Avonmouth and Royal Edward docks, brought the water acreage to 21, and 110 acres of dockland surrounding it.

Avonmouth became part of the City of Bristol under boundary extensions in 1895. By 1904 all the land between Clifton and Avonmouth had been absorbed by the city and since that date – and contrary to popular myth – Avonmouth has been neither town nor village, but a suburb of Bristol with no more autonomy than any other suburb.

Sadly, within fifteeen years of starting trading, it became obvious that Avonmouth failed to measure up to the vision of its promoters. Many transatlantic liners were far too big to enter port and in July 1900 the City Council decided to do something about it. The marshlands of Avonmouth would be disturbed once again ...

The m.v. *Birmingham City*, 5571 tons, at Hosegood's Mill in 1955: acquired secondhand by the Bristol City Line in 1950, and sold in 1963 when the new *Montreal City* came into service. The Haven Master's launch *Research*, in foreground, was bought in 1952 and sold to a retired admiral in 1973 when the twin-engined, echo-sounding launch *Mathew* replaced her. The *Research* rotted away at Sharpness Dock. Hosegood's Mill was constructed in 1936.

Nice to see you ... although Liverpool was the home port of Ellerman's liner *City of Bristol*, this 8459-ton vessel was a popular visitor, especially when the Charles Hill liner *Bristol City* was in dock at the same time.   Here, she discharges general cargo at L Shed, Old Dock, early in 1968.

A fine pair ... two well known ships occupied the far corner of Avonmouth Dock during November, 1968: the *Bristol City*, 5887 tons, and *Athelmonarch*, 10,937 tons.   In the background, at L Shed, is the 4275-ton *Fana*.

Black treacle and black smoke are discharged together as the 10,924-ton tanker, *Athellaird*, pumps Cuban molasses ashore at the Old Dock during February, 1969.

The 7444-grt Strick liner *Farsistan* is about to sail from a busy Avonmouth Dock on 3 April, 1969.   Behind the tug *Sea Challenge* is Spillers' Mill, closed 20 March, 1980, and demolished soon afterwards.   The 102-foot *Sea Challenge* came into service on 12 January, 1968 to replace the beautiful steam tug *Bristolian* which served the Port for fifty-six years.

Two bows and a stern ... traffic at the Old Dock in June 1970.

Little and large ... a 1598-ton Liverpool coaster shares the Old Dock repair jetty with a 10,929-ton Indian cargo liner in the early-1970s.

Paul's Mill at Avonmouth Dock receives grain from coasters eighteen months before demolition at the end of 1972. The silo to the left remains, and is now occupied by grain merchants Charles E. Ford Ltd.

Terminal force – the m.v. *Apollo*, 1254 tons, loads cargo for Dublin at N Berth early in 1973. This container terminal was opened on 11 August, 1969, and replaced the Bristol Steam Navigation Company's Irish berth at M Shed, City Docks. Operated by 23 men, it was for over ten years the only container terminal at Avonmouth Docks. Increased competition, and a disruptive tally clerks' dispute at the Dublin terminal, closed the service in April, 1980, ending 158 years of regular trading.

Four across ... much seems to be happening at the Old Dock in the autumn of 1976 as the 8230-ton *Westmorland* discharges at L Shed, the *Gladstone Star*, 10,635 tons, and *Michurinsk*, 5518 tons, occupy the repair jetty, and a coaster delivers a consignment of grain to Hosegood's silo.   In the foreground are T. R. Brown's tugs *Ernest Brown* and *Leader*.

Last lock-out ... just three months short of its centenary, the old lock at Avonmouth Dock was closed and sealed off from the open sea.   The last ship to pass through the 454 feet by 70 feet entrance was the 1254-ton *Apollo* on 14 November, 1976.   The first ship through the lock when the Dock opened on 24 February, 1877 had been another Bristol Steam Navigation vessel, the 1021-ton paddle steamer *Juno*.

This south east corner of Avonmouth Dock was an early-1890s extension, around fifteen years after the dock was opened, and added 1500 feet of linear quayage.   In January, 1977 the 6753-ton Russian ship *Dorogobuzh* is pictured discharging 8165 tons of feed and grain from Corpus Christi, Texas directly into the Charles E. Ford granary.   This berth was formerly occupied by Paul's Mill, most of which was demolished in 1972.

To the left, the m.v. *Echo*, 1241 tons, loads containers for Dublin at Bristol Seaways' N Berth.   This berth was for decades home to Elders & Fyffes' banana boats until the trade ceased in February, 1967.   Bristol Steam Navigation Company transferred here in August, 1969 from A and M Sheds in the City Docks.

This handsome Houlder liner of 9234 gross tons is towed from the Royal Edward Dock into Avonmouth Dock in spring, 1977 for minor maintenance work.

Quayside colonnade – the BOCM Mill, formerly Robinsons, on the waterfront at the Avonmouth Dock, falls into disrepair in the late-1970s, just before demolition. BOCM relocated to the Portbury side of the Avon in the early-1980s with a smaller, but fully computerized mill, and far fewer staff.

Big stars ... these majestic Blue Star liners, *Rockhampton Star*, 11,872 tons, and *Queensland Star*, 9,911 tons, made an impressive sight when they were in the Old Dock in 1978 for engine room maintenance. Pictured, foreground, are a bunch of T. R. Brown's barges moored at BOCM's berth. One, *The Shoots*, named after a narrow channel in the Severn, was later converted into a floating restaurant at Hotwells.

Tugs *Sea Volunteer* and *Sea Merrimac*, 163 tons – surplus to requirements after the merger of C. J. King & Sons Ltd and Cory Ship Towage Ltd on 1 February, 1983 – were laid up in the Old Dock before being sold.   Astern is the Black Star Line's *Kulpawn River*, 7356 grt.

Flour for Ethopia ... Band Aid fever swept the nation during the mid-1980s, and Bristol played its part when this 1599-ton Cypriot vessel loaded provisions at L Shed in Avonmouth Dock.

Bulgarian bonus ... a badly needed service was introduced to the Old Dock in March, 1987 when So-Mat, the major Bulgarian haulage company, established weekly voyages to St Nazaire, Limassol and Bourgas on the Black Sea.   Two 15,373-ton, roll-on ships, *Mercandian Ocean* and *Mercandian Universe*, both had deck space for 150 trailers.   Contract difficulties elsewhere meant the trade was short-lived and, like other exciting new ventures, is now only a memory.

Shifting sands – after eighty years, the dredging of sand and gravel from the bed of the Bristol Channel and discharging it around the City Docks was transferred to Avonmouth in 1990.   Half a million tons are brought ashore annually by British Dredging Aggregates and United Marine Aggregates.   These two companies have now established their own berths at opposite ends of the Old Dock.

The sand dredger *City of Bristol*, 1027 tons, here discharges its cargo at the United Marine compound in 1990. The old Avonmouth Dock entrance, closed in 1976 – but thankfully not totally landfilled – provides ideal accommodation to these small sand vessels: a trade not lost to Bristol – simply shifted from one dock to another.

Port peelers... In 1884, Bristol acquired control of the two rivermouth docks at Portishead and Avonmouth, thereby ending damaging competition between the City Docks and these two new upstarts and, in so doing, triggered off the City's gradual boundary expansion to the shores of the Bristol Channel. During the summer of 1984 the Port Police Department decided to create a large cake and set it atop the Haven Master's launch *Mathew*, to mark, not only the occasion of the Port's anniversary, but their own century as a Force to be reckoned with. The actual icing on the cake, however, came when the Float copped first prize at the Bristol Water Festival in June of that year. The Victorian-clad bobbies, pictured raising their hats to ten decades of dedicated duty and achievement are: John House, Pat Comer, Keith Woods, Danny Cooney, and Bill Knight. Crowd pleasers, one and all...

Portishead Dock

Portishead Dock, built primarily for the wheat and barley trade in 1879, was by 1969 almost completely dominated by the Albright & Wilson phosphorous works on the South Wharf and by the giant power station which
occupied the north side of the 16-acre dock.   The 440 feet by 66 feet locks can be seen in the foreground as a
large coaster vacates them for the open sea.

[overleaf] Peaceful Portishead – this 1968 view illustrates the relative quiet enjoyed at Bristol's smallest dock
system – in contrast to the general bustle at Avonmouth and the City Docks.   The power station, on the north
side of the quay, was constructed during the early to mid-1950s on a section of quay occupied, until 1952, by a
granary and grain storage sheds.   The South Wharf was extended and modernised in 1952-53 to provide
additional timber stacking grounds, and a customized berth to serve the newly-installed Albright & Wilson
phosphorous factory.

Port expansion fever among Bristol merchants soared to such high temperatures during the 1860s that it culminated, a decade later, in not one new dock, but two. Civic leaders, along with maritime entrepreneurs, had long been divided as to which side of the Avon's mouth would be more suitable for dockland development. Speculation therefore saw rail links forged to both Portishead to the south and Avonmouth to the north.

By the late 1860s, port expansionists had established themselves in two camps – each hoping they would be riding the gravy train as they journeyed to the open sea with men and construction equipment along their respective rail tracks. The Bristol Port and Channel Dock Company broke the ground first by starting work on the construction of Avonmouth Dock in 1868. Two years later, The Portishead Pier and Railway Company was granted permission to construct an undertaking of similar proportions at the end of its line in the small Somerset town. Serious delays during excavation resulted from financial difficulties and the collapse, and eventual rebuilding, of a 350-feet long section of quay wall.

Portishead Dock opened its gates to the world on 28 June, 1879. A small party of dignitaries locked into the 16 acres of impounded water aboard the little pleasure steamer *Lyn*. Few people lined the quays and in contrast to all the excitement at the Avonmouth Dock ceremony over two years earlier, it was a modest beginning. As a result Bristol now had three competing dock systems.

It was unfortunate that the opening of the rivermouth docks coincided with a temporary slump in world shipping movements. To attract business from one another, the dock owners reduced their charges to unprofitable levels. This self-defeating move lasted until September, 1884 when the cash-strapped Avonmouth and Portishead companies were forced to surrender their docks to the Bristol Docks Committee for £550,000 – half the original cost of constructing them. Bristol was one port again.

Portishead Dock in its early days was well-equipped and included a granary with all the necessary elevating machinery, an open wharf for timber-laden vessels, and travelling cranes and extensive shed accommodation – all of which were linked to mainline rail connections. Storage tanks were constructed also in 1908 by the Anglo-Saxon Oil Company on a $3^1/_2$-acre site to supply the ever-increasing demands for petroleum spirit to those new-fangled horseless carriages that were beginning to make their presence felt across the nation's highways.

The two rivermouth docks had barely opened before their ability to cope with the increased size and design of modern shipping was being questioned – the locks were quite simply too small to handle the fast-growing Atlantic liner trade. Throughout the 1890s, proposals were made for major dock extension towards the Portbury marshes. But for the woefully inadequate entrance lock at Portishead, these plans might well have been realised as an alternative to the eventual construction of the Royal Edward Dock. The primary object of building docks at the rivermouth in the first place was to accommodate vessels too large to negotiate the River Avon. With the width of the Portishead entrance, only four feet greater than the lock at Cumberland Basin, the advantages must have been marginal and barely worth the enormous capital investment. Such short-sighted planning was to destroy the original dream.

The Portishead dock measures 360 feet across and is 1800 feet in length, with a water depth of 29 feet. In all probability the largest ship to enter port was the Australian liner, *Everton Grange*, of 7202 tons, back in 1908. With a length of 490 feet, fifty feet longer than the lock, she had to pass through into the dock on the high-tide level so that the inner and outer gates could remain open at the same time.

Although the dock estate totalled 76 acres, Portishead was to remain the poor relation in the Port of Bristol network and was relegated to a low-profile status for most of its active existence, although the two world wars brought increased trade and it assumed some importance as a relief to the overstretched docks at Avonmouth. The timber business remained constant at Portishead over the years but otherwise the emphasis changed gradually away from grain and gasoline to phosphates, coal and finally woodpulp – a trade transferred from the City Docks in 1970.

The big decline started in 1976 with the closure of the pulp terminal. This was followed closely by the phasing out of the power station, and when the Albright and Wilson phosphorous works ceased to import raw materials its fate was sealed. On 8 February, 1990, the m.v. *Bright Pioneer* (formerly *Albright Pioneer*) slipped her moorings and sailed on the evening tide. With the gates closed behind her the lock gatemen switched off the power, locked their office and went home. Portishead Dock had ceased trading.

Portishead had served Bristol and the West Country faithfully, but quietly, for 110 years. This once great enterprise which fired up the hearts and minds of Victorian visionaries now rests in a state of desolation awaiting, perhaps, transformation to a more prosaic role – providing recreation for expensive waterfront homes ...

The 2175-ton tanker *Chailey* has discharged her cargo into the power station while, opposite, the 6646-ton *Arthur Albright* waits to off-load her final shipment of phosphates into the Albright & Wilson works during September, 1968. Designed to carry the maximum cargo into Portishead, the 414 feet by 57 feet vessel first arrived on 21 March, 1961 with 9500 tons of phosphate from Tampa, Florida, and for over seven years was the largest regular visitor to the dock.

Lady in waiting ... after over forty years maintaining deep-water levels at Bristol's three dock systems, the old dredger *B. D. Clifton* was, early in 1968, laid up at Portishead while waiting to be towed to Newport for scrap. Astern of the doomed vessel were two Osborne and Wallis colliers: *Hotwells*, 499 tons, and *St Vincent* at 484 tons. Other ships in the O & W fleet, used to transport Welsh coal to Portishead Power Station, included *Colston*, *Druid Stoke*, *Brandon*, *Downleaze* and *Salcombe*.

A bright pair ... when the 1953-built Albright & Wilson factory was converted to a terminal for finished product phosphorous in 1968, two specially designed ships were built to transport the phosphorous from Long Harbor, Newfoundland to the Portishead storage tanks. Motor vessels *Albright Pioneer*, 6789 tons, and *Albright Explorer*, 6870 tons, became, at 412 feet by 58 feet, the largest regular traders to use the dock. They stayed in service for 21 years until the production furnaces at Long Harbor were closed in 1989, and the Port of Bristol link was severed.

Dock of desolation ... after one hundred years of trading with the world, Portishead Dock finally closed to shipping on 8 February, 1990 after the *Bright Pioneer* sailed on the evening tide. Very few signs of life were evident when this aerial photograph was taken in June, 1993. The quays had been stripped, Albright & Wilson's phosphorous factory had all but disappeared, and little remained of the power station – once such a potent landmark with its four 350-foot chimneys dominating the skyline.

Portishead was always the poor relation in the Port of Bristol family of docks and with so many erstwhile dock systems lying idle around Britain's coasts, no-one was surprised when the final curtain fell.

Down she comes ... it was all over in a flash as this 350-foot chimney came tumbling down in September, 1981.
Within a few years all four redundant power station chimneys were demolished, dramatically changing the
Portishead skyline.

Change of scene ... the 1000-ton *Scol Spirit* discharges 2400 tons of Swedish woodpulp into open rail trucks at the Portishead Pulp Terminal during the summer of 1972. Commissioned in 1970, this terminal replaced the City Docks as the centre for the import of woodpulp. The cranes had come from Bathurst Wharf in 1969, where they had long been used for handling woodpulp. The terminal closed at the end of 1976, owing in part to the availability of more home-produced pulp, but in the main to the decline of St Anne's Board Mills.

The Royal Edward Dock

'I declare the Royal Edward Dock now open,' boomed Edward VII, and crowds cheered the fanfare of trumpets and the barking of guns from a cruiser moored outside the dock. It was 9 July, 1908 and after six years of construction, a new ocean dock – built to maintain Bristol's position as a major port during the twentieth century – was finally opened.

The King continued: 'The splendid dock, which I gladly permit to be called by my name, will, I am sure, prove a powerful stimulus to your trade and so increase the wealth and prosperity of your city. This dock, constructed at great expense by vast labour, will be capable of receiving through its fine entrance piers the largest ships of all nations.'

During the 1890s trade between Great Britain and North America was increasing, as was the size of the Atlantic liners. The existing entrance lock at the Avonmouth Dock – opened only a few years earlier in 1877 – was by now hopelessly inadequate to accommodate these larger vessels, and commercial groups were anxious to see steps taken to match dock expansion elsewhere. By 1894 controversy raged between those who favoured a completely new dock, others who demanded the dockizing of the Avon, and a group led by Alderman Proctor Baker who were fearful of jeopardising existing investments in the City Docks and therefore argued against any form of rivermouth expansion.

In September, 1897 the proponents of an enlarged port won the day, and plans were put forward for a new dock with an entrance lock of 850 feet by 80 feet. It was three years before the City Council approved the scheme which was to be known as the Royal Edward Dock. The delay proved fortuitous as by then the Atlantic mail ships were so large that locks measuring 875 feet long by 100 feet wide were adopted.

In January, 1901 the proposal was endorsed by Bristol citizens when a town poll registered a three-to-one majority in favour. An application to Parliament was made and in March the next year the Prince and Princess of Wales travelled to Bristol for the ground-breaking ceremony. The Prince was invited to set in motion a steam shovel which scooped up the first of more than 3 1/2 million cubic yards of earth that had to be removed before the ambitious undertaking could be transformed into a recognisable dock.

The site of the Royal Edward Dock was flat grassland only slighly above high water level. The ground around the dock had to be raised and, after a new coast line was created by reclaiming hundreds of acres from the sea, the low-lying land was built up with the excavated soil. Once the new coastline was established, worked started on the two piers which stretch out into the channel as guiding arms for incoming vessels. The South Pier is 900 feet long and the North, 1200 feet. On each extremity is a lighthouse which, as they are 550 feet apart, allows ample room for ships, assisted by a Bristol pilot and tugboats, to pass between on course for the entrance lock.

A main basin was constructed 1000 feet across from east to west, with similar dimensions north to south. Extending from the south-east was a 500-foot arm, 250 feet wide, from which a junction cut, 525 feet in length and 85 feet wide, connected the old Avonmouth Dock with its larger neighbour. At the north end of the basin, provision was made for the construction of two extension arms if future trade made this necessary.

Another notable feature was a dry dock with the same dimensions as the entrance lock and running parallel with it.   On the eastern quays O and P two-storey transit sheds, each equipped with half a dozen roof-top cranes, were built, and a large granary behind dominated the area. To the south, a single-storey corrugated building, 1000 feet long, was erected to handle exports. Divided into two sections it became Q and S sheds. Three months after the official opening, the Royal Edward Dock was ready to trade with the world.

The massive expansion of the Port of Bristol between 1809 and 1909 contributed greatly to the city's prosperity. The Floating Harbour had been built and by 1895 contained 4 miles of modern paved quayage; Avonmouth and Portishead Docks provided much expanded facilities; and by the time the Royal Edward Dock had opened for business, the population of Bristol had risen ten-fold, with natural growth and boundary changes, and the city now covered an area 23 times greater than a century earlier.

The first commercial vessel to use the new dock was s.s. *Dorset* of the Bristol-Australia line. The steamer started loading on Monday, 19 October, 1908 with general cargo for Sydney, Brisbane, Melbourne and Adelaide. The first shipment into the dock – 15,000 cases of canned fruit from San Francisco – arrived on Saturday, 14 November in the same year, aboard the French steamer, *Admiral Magon*. It was the first consignment of that class of goods to be handled at the Port of Bristol and the ship was discharged in one day. It was now full steam ahead for the future ...

From 1914 to 1918 the Royal Edward and Avonmouth Docks served as an embarkation centre for troops, horses, tanks, ammunition and supplies *en route* to the European War. When hostilities ceased, the veil of secrecy which had enveloped port activities for more than four years was lifted, and trade returned to normal.

By 1913, the escalating demand for petroleum products led to negotiations between the Bristol Docks Committee and the Anglo-Mexico Oil Company to provide oil terminal facilities. Installations had existed on the riverside of Avonmouth Dock since 1889 and at Portishead since 1908 but there was limited scope for future expansion and for the size of ships they could accommodate. The Western Arm, used then as a timber pond, was the obvious site to build a jetty for tanker discharge and there was ample land between the dock and the River Severn to build storage tanks. The Timber Pond became the Oil Basin and over several decades expanded gradually until the early 1960s, by which time it boasted eight modern tanker berths.

In the early 1920s, the Port of Bristol required additional general cargo berths and work started on the Eastern Arm extension in 1924. This was to run parallel with the Western Arm and offer six working berths in a section of dock measuring 1700 feet long by 400 feet wide. On 23 May, 1928, the Elders & Fyffes liner, *Bayano*, with the Prince of Wales manning the helm, sailed into the newly-created 21 acres of water to break a long red, white and blue ribbon stretched across the entrance.

Also completed that year were U and V transit sheds and the No 3 Granary which occupied the eastern side of what, for a short period, became known as the Prince of Wales Extension. Three open berths were developed at the West Wharf opposite. In 1941 the Eastern Arm was enlarged again adding two more berths to the West Wharf with the five-storey W shed and open X berth adorning the opposite bank. The Royal Edward Dock now had nine waterfront transit sheds, eight open general cargo berths, a CWS Mill and granary section, plus an oil basin. It was well equipped to handle the busy years which followed the end of the Second World War through to the early 1970s.

The 1960s saw major investment in modernising and improving facilities at the Royal Edward and Avonmouth Docks. West Wharf was repaved and strengthened and the Oil Basin was reconstructed; O and P sheds had their Edwardian verandahs removed and more powerful cranes were installed. New diesel locomotives finally replaced the steam engines, the modern L transit shed was constructed at the Old Dock on the site of the ancient K & M shed, while new cranes ousted the old everywhere, with the Kangaroos at West Wharf 5, Transporter at West Wharf 4, and the slimline Blue Streaks representing the notable examples. Two modern dredgers, s.d. *Severn* and b.d. *Clifton* replaced elderly namesakes; the Signal Station was commissioned and St Andrews Canteen built, while the amenity block opened, offering dockers facilities to shower and wash the lampblack or lousy meal dust from their bodies at the end of the working day. A conveyor system replaced the old ropeway between West Wharf 5 and the National Smelting Company capable of transporting 1000 tons of raw material an hour from ship to factory.   No 5 Granary, perhaps the greatest investment of all and certainly one of the tallest buildings in Bristol, was completed in 1966 and added 30,000 tons of storage capacity to an over-stretched Grain Section.

Most major oil companies updated their pipeline and storage facilities and by the end of the 1960s the port offered very efficient discharge methods to the numerous British and foreign fleets which then operated.

There was a wonderful working atmosphere.   Small vessels – tugs, barges, grain elevators, dredgers and clinker working boats – moved from one berth to another, usually between tides, and such was the shipping activity at high water that outward-bound coasters and barges normally made their way to the locks around three hours to flow.   Rail traffic served every berth, and long lines of BD trucks snaked their way around miles of rail-road, having right of way over vehicular traffic and the hundreds of cycling workers using the 7 miles of internal highways.   An estimated 6000 people worked in the docks, many in the nine provender and flour mills located around the port.

Employees' social life perked up with the building of two new clubhouses: the Sports and Social Club at Shirehampton for PBA staff, and, at Welsh Back, the Dockers Club replaced inadequate club facilities at Bedminster.

Trade continued to flourish as the high-rolling 1960s made way for the '70s, but at the end of that decade things would be altogether different.   The British merchant fleets were in decline.   Built-to-pattern general cargo ships had to compete with purpose-built, space-efficient vessels, often constructed for specific commodities. Specialised cargoes required different methods of discharge and the PBA updated several berths to keep pace with the fast flowing tide of change.   The sight of the red ensign fluttering in the breeze became rare through the 1980s, with Greek, Russian and flag-of-convenience vessels dominating the Royal Edward waterfront.

The changes were equally dramatic in the adjacent working areas.   By the end of the 1980s long familiar land-marks such as the Cold Stores, Spillers' Mill, Granaries 3 and 4, Jefferies' workshops, C and D warehouses and the central canteen had been torn down, leaving acres of wasteland.   The sound of train whistles, the sight of grain, tobacco and log barges, the pumphouse siren and the tinkling of bicycle bells – all were now experiences of the past.

Even so, and despite the emphasis on Portbury during the early 1990s, the Avonmouth Docks system has increased its trade and the total tonnage handled during 1994 was almost double that handled at Royal Portbury Dock in the same year.

The main commodities dealt with at the Royal Edward Dock in the mid-1990s have been bulk liquids discharged into the Oil Basin pipelines, timber for Denholm Shipping, scrap metal for Bird's shredding terminal, concentrates for Commonwealth Smelting works, cement for Castle and house coal for E H. Bennett Ltd.   In addition to all this, Bell Lines opened a container terminal in November, 1993, bringing with it a welcome morale boost and a startling change to the appearance of the West Wharf.

As with Royal Portbury, The Bristol Port Company is anxious to attract new customers to the Avonmouth side of the river and as a result some of the original transit sheds might have to be removed to allow new open wharves to be developed for the handling and storage of specific cargoes.

The Royal Edward Dock deserves a brighter future.   It has served Bristol well.   When it opened in 1908, King Edward VII called it a 'splendid dock'.   It is splendid still – and may its splendour live on.

73

Rea's slickest and most modern tug of the 1950s: the powerful *Westgarth* tows the 1937-built tanker *Regent Panther*, 9556 tons, out of the locks in December, 1954.

Liberty ship *City of Chelmsford*, 7267 tons, and *Clan Chisholm*, 7870 tons, had to share X berth during January, 1955 – a month which began with 36 ships in Avonmouth Docks, 20 berthed in the City Docks, and eight more anchored in Walton Bay anxious to come into port.   Astern of the *Clan* is Donaldson liner *Salacia*, a regular visitor on the North Atlantic run and sold to breakers in 1960.   PBA grain barges are moored at the batter, along with the 1936 fire boat *Endres Gane*, replaced in 1968 by the more efficient, but less attractive, *Aquanaut*.   Many survivors of the 2709 Liberty ships built during the Second World War were frequent visitors to Avonmouth Docks in the 1950s.

Clan MacTaggart, 8035 tons, discharges a cargo of tea into the roof hatches of P Shed in 1955, while another Clan liner is berthed at Q Shed.   The verandah and roof-top cranes at P Shed were removed in 1969 to provide more quay working space.

Old favourite at Q Shed in 1955 – one of the best-loved ships ever to frequent Avonmouth Docks was this 1926-built Elders & Fyffes banana/passenger liner *Ariguani*, 6878 tons. After thirty years, which included active duty in the Second World War convoys, this 425 feet by 54 feet lovely old lady left the Royal Edward Dock for the breakers at Briton Ferry.   She sheared about between King Road and the Holms in an alarming manner and ended up with her bow pointing back towards Bristol …a sad day for both ship and city.

75

Banana beauty ... another port favourite was the s.s. *Cavina*, 6907 tons, pictured at the North Wall in 1955. A year later, this 1924-built Elders & Fyffes liner sailed for Hong Kong and was scrapped in 1958.

The steam tug *Merrimac*, one of the most attractive of C. J. King's fleet, tows a Norwegian ex-Liberty ship *K. C. Rogeraes*, 5220 tons, into the Royal Edward Dock in the summer of 1955. The buildings either side of the locks have gone – as, sadly, has the *Merrimac*, which served the Port from 1919 until 1963.

The magic of steam ... puffing past S Shed in 1955, this Port locomotive, along with around thirty others, added much to the bustle of activity and atmosphere special to Avonmouth Docks before the 1970 trade patterns changed waterfront life for ever.   The shrill whistle of these Bristol-built iron horses could be heard throughout the docks.

Many were named after suburbs – *Henbury* is one that survives at the Bristol Industrial Museum at Prince's Wharf.   By 6 August, 1965, the line ran out for these old steamers and diesel dominated the Port's internal rail network for the final years of its existence.

Wharf of activity ... Henderson liner *Martaban*, 5740 tons, Blue Funnel's *Troilus*, 7287 tons, and the 8035-ton *Clan MacTaggart* were just three ships filling the West Wharf in 1956 – years before the arrival of the 9-ton Transporter and Kangaroo cranes which, in the 1960s, changed the face of West Wharf 4 and 5.

USA-bound ... this 1941-built Donaldson liner *Calgaria*, 8418 tons, heads out into the Bristol Channel passing the 1919-built suction dredger *Severn* during a summer evening in 1956.   The Donaldson Line service was similar to Bristol City Line's: regular sailings between Bristol and the Eastern Seaboard.   The 199-foot long *Severn* served the Port for forty-seven years by keeping the approaches free of silt and mud until being replaced by a larger dredger of the same name in 1966.

Record breaker ... named after a wonderful city, this 667 feet by 85 feet oil tanker of 21,877 gross tons, arrived on 18 April, 1960 – the largest vessel to enter the Oil Basin to that date. She returned in July, 1968 with motor spirit from Bahrein.

Two famous ship-repairing names – Jefferies and Mount-stuart – shared dry dock duties and facilities in the 1960s, when this 9986-ton Federal liner was about to be worked on.

Gloucester City, 5581 tons, loads exports at S Shed for Baltimore on 26 March, 1968 – her final voyage as a Bristol City liner before being sold to a Greek shipping line after nearly fourteen years' service to Charles Hill and her home port.   At R Shed in the autumn of 1954, fresh from the builder, newly painted, and as yet unblemished by the dark moods of the Western Ocean, ablaze with bunting from stem to stern ... she looked slicker than a brook trout.

A handsome line up ... Berths X, W, V and U in the Eastern Arm are all fully occupied by these Anchor, Indian, Brocklebank and Bank liners during the spring of 1968.   The m.v. *Lossiebank*, 8519 tons, discharges tobacco overside to Benjamin Perry barges.

Gordon Phillips, loading New Zealand lamb into a refrigerated truck in 1968, was one of more than 100 dockers affectionately known as 'Meat Flies', who enjoyed working with meat and other frozen food from New Zealand and Australia. Many toiled in the icy chambers of the Royal Edward Cold Stores – known as 'The Pot' – while others sorted meat to mark in the warmer, but draughty, tween-decks of O and P Sheds.

These happy dockers are about to land a hoist of New Zealand butter in the tween-deck of O Shed during March, 1968. From here it was sorted to mark before being transferred to the adjacent Royal Edward Cold Stores via a connecting conveyor system.

Between tides – tugs at rest outside the Royal Edward Dry Dock during the summer of 1968 until, come high water, they broke moorings around three hours to flow to tow some of the 5430 ships which came into port that year. Berthed at T Shed is the 10,936-ton Federal liner, *Essex*.

With only three feet to spare either side, the m.v. *Chennai Ookkam*, 24,365 tons, inches her way through the 100-foot wide Royal Edward lock entrance at 5 a.m. on 21 June, 1968 before berthing at West Wharf 3 with a cargo of packaged timber. This was the largest ship to enter the Port of Bristol to that date, breaking a fifty-three-year record held by the s.s. *Rotterdam*, 24,149 tons, which berthed at P Shed in 1915.

The old roof-top cranes discharge New Zealand dairy produce from the Federal Shipping Company's *Essex*, 10,936 gross tons, at P Shed in the summer of 1968 as the little dock tug *Salisbury* steams by. Built in 1943, and acquired by Benjamin Perry & Sons Ltd in 1949, the *Salisbury* was originally named *BP11* and had a taller funnel. She was sold to the Laxey Towing Company, Isle of Man, after the collapse of Bristol Seaways' Dublin/Bristol service in April, 1980.

Looking as a ship ought to look, this 7145-ton Strick liner cut a striking pose as she basked in the evening sun at West Wharf 4 during the summer of 1968.

Between the piers ... Rea's tug *Falgarth* waits to re-enter port; the *Severn* is busily dredging the entrance channel, and the 12,605-ton *Tasmania Star* looks ready to clear the Royal Edward locks and head for open waters on this summer evening in 1968.

Quaint, perhaps, when viewed alongside modern container stacking methods, but this side loader attracted attention in August, 1968 as it stood by at S Shed to assist the 7643-ton *Coventry City* load a small number of boxes. The newer Bristol City liners, which came into service in the mid-1960s, had facilities to ship containers but, despite all the tall-talking about Bristol's future in the fast-growing world of containerization, there simply wasn't enough hard-standing acreage within Avonmouth Docks to translate into solid reality.

The elegant Shaw Savill liner *Gothic*, 15,900 tons, was lucky to be in port on 29 October, 1968 after a severe fire in the Indian Ocean when seven lives were lost. The boom in the foreground, for many decades separating the waters of the Oil Basin from the rest of the Royal Edward Dock, was dismantled and put to the torch in the early-1990s.

The graceful *Port Brisbane*, 11,942 tons, is temporarily berthed in the Oil Basin while undergoing engine room maintenance in December, 1968.

The 11,347-grt tanker *Border Terrier*, owned by Lowland Tanker Company of Newcastle, being towed towards the Oil Basin from the turning basin with a full cargo of petroleum products during December, 1968.

The world's largest refrigerated vessel *Port Chalmers*, 16,283 gross registered tons, receives a check-up in dry dock after her maiden voyage in January, 1969, before returning to New Zealand with Rover and Jaguar cars.

Success symbol ... many international ports owned a helicopter in the 1960s. Bristol's was purchased, ostensibly, for observing flotsam at the Port approaches. It was, however, used primarily to offer VIPs and potential customers a bird's eye view of dockside facilities and the port environs. It was a casualty of financial belt-tightening when, in the early 1970s, the PBA accounts drifted into deficit.

An old friend returns ... little over a year after the m.v. *New York City*, 5603 tons, was sold to Greek shipping interests, the former Bristol City liner was back in her home port. Renamed *Avis Ornis*, the 1956-built vessel berthed at T Shed on 24 April, 1969.

Long gone ... all the buildings to the left of this 1969 photograph have been demolished – the Channel Mill, Pearce's Mill and the 1908 export sheds R, Q and S, sacrificed to make room for modern transit sheds and a lumber storage area during the early-1970s.   At the bottom right, O Shed – another 1908 original – was scheduled to be torn down at the close of 1996 to facilitate berth redevelopment.

Running parallel ... the Royal Edward locks and dry dock are side by side, with identical dimensions of 875 feet by 100 feet. This aerial shot illustrates how close together they are with the 9390-ton Liberian-registered *Master Nicos* in the locks, and Andrew Weir's *Irisbank*, 10,349 tons, undergoing repairs in the dry dock during March, 1989. The oil tanks beyond were being built for a new Shell-Mex terminal – these were torn down in 1993, for Shell to share facilities with Esso Petroleum at Holesmouth, just outside the dock limits.

This 15,761-ton Danish bulker, berthed at No 3 Granary, discharged 10,000 tons of grain in March, 1969 and was typical of the ships using this deep-water berth at the time. The PBA tug *Cabot*, 98 tons, served the port well for twenty-two years and was always kept shipshape and Bristol fashion by skipper George Sewell and crew.

Granaries galore ... overhead conveyors, underground tunnels – all were part of the extensive Port granary system when grain imports averaged around one million tons a year.   The 13,825-ton Norwegian carrier *Bulk Enterprise* is pictured during March, 1969 with suction elevators busily helping themselves to her cargo in holds 2 and 4.   This waterfront is very different today as bulk carriers arrive at the former No 3 Granary and CWS berths to load consignments of scrap metal.

Empty and out ... the graceful lines of this 9300-ton Indian Steamship liner in the spring sunshine as she is towed out of port on 3 April, 1969, following her discharge of a cargo of tea at W Shed.

First lock ... a miscellany of large and small craft – Tewkesbury grain barges, Bristol Steam Navigation's *Milo* and Lambert Brothers' 7701-ton m.v. *Dunster* (formerly *Temple Lane*) fill the Royal Edward 875 feet by 100 feet locks, while waiting to sail at two hours to flow one evening in 1969.

Bristol City liner m.v. *Halifax City*, 6533 tons, berthing alongside an East German freighter at X Berth during April, 1969 while waiting her turn to be loaded with exports for the USA.   Like her sister *Montreal City*, the *Halifax* was sold in 1972 to a Bangkok shipping company.   Also pictured are two British Waterways barges and their tug *Resolute*.

Virginia tobacco offloaded to shore and barge from the m.v. *Toronto City*, 7643 tons, at V Shed in June, 1969 – when U and V Sheds possessed four roof-top cranes apiece. Commodities were then landed either to quayside or into the transit sheds through any number of roof hatches. The *Toronto City* was built in 1966 and, like her sister *Coventry City*, was specially constructed for the Atlantic trade.

Both ships were on long-term charter to Bristol City Line from the Bibby Line of Liverpool which, in 1972, acquired a controlling interest in the Bristol company, and closed down the Bristol/Eastern Seaboard operation. On 12 February, 1972 the *Toronto City* sailed to Hamburg after arriving at Avonmouth eight days earlier with the very last consignment of Bristol City Line cargo from New York. Ninety three years of Bristol shipping history was brought to a close.

Outward bound ... logs for Lydney in Ashmead barges squeeze past the USA-bound, 6502-ton *Montreal City*, as the Royal Edward lock begins to fill with outgoing vessels during August, 1969. Less than three years later, the *Montreal City* – the third ship to bear the name – was sold to the Thai Maritime Navigation Company of Bangkok and renamed *Ratchaburi*. While rubber was loaded in South Thailand in March, 1973, a fire swept the ten-year old ship and she sank in Pattani Bay.

A hoist of New Zealand lamb is discharged at O Shed during 1969 from the 15,067-ton Shaw Savill liner *Ceramic*.   A decade later this long established refrigerated trade was containerised and lost to Tilbury and Liverpool.

The first lock-out filling up on a September tide in 1969 with the m.v. *Milo*, 991 tons, making one of her last voyages under the Bristol Steam Navigation flag – she was sold the following month and renamed *Saint Angus*.   Ahead of her is another Company ship *Echo*, 1241 tons, and moving towards the outer gates are pilot cutters *Sally Organ* and *Nancy Raymond*.

The 6502-ton Bristol City liner *Montreal City* loads general cargo for the USA at Q Shed while the Eastern Arm hosts an impressive number of ships during the spring of 1970.

In March, 1970 the 90-ton *Nonsuch* – an exact replica of a seventeenth-century square-rigged ketch – was hoisted aboard the m.v. *Bristol City* by the 150-ton floating crane Bristol Giant in a specially constructed cradle for shipment to Canada. The *Nonsuch* played a big part in the tercentenary celebrations of the Hudson Bay Company. The 1959-built *Bristol City*, 5887 tons, flagship of the Bristol City Line, was sold in September, 1970 to a Panamanian-based company and renamed *Angelos Gabrieke*.

These boatmen are dwarfed as they stand by to assist with the ropes of the 16,969-ton bulk carrier *Demeterton*, which is leaving port after discharging Australian barley at No 3 Granary in May, 1970.

C. J. King's most beautiful tug *Sea Queen*, 244 tons, approaches the Royal Edward locks in May, 1970 with the Liberian tanker *World Sea*, 12,843 tons, under tow.

'We've got the ships, we've got the men, we've got the money too' ... the words of that patriotic song could well serve the Port of Bristol during this busy spell in the summer of 1970. Take a long look ... we're not likely again to see triple and double-berthing along the Eastern Arm, with more ships waiting to dock out at Walton Bay.

A pair of pretty Blue-Flues – *Antenor*, 7672 tons, and *Cyclops*, 7416 tons – double up at W Shed during August, 1970.   The Blue Funnel Line possessed some of the most majestic ships to use the Port – always maintained to a high standard, their distinctive features and graceful lines added a touch of class to the Royal Edward Dock.

After the Second World War, the line shipped around 30,000 tons of canned goods and general cargo annually through Bristol from the Far East.   This ended in September, 1971 when the Blue Funnel Line decided to confine their UK activity to Liverpool and Birkenhead.   A few years later, like many other British shipping lines, they had gone altogether.

Ron Heard and Paul England find time to smile at the camera as they help load a large shipment of coffee to BD open rail trucks at W Shed in 1970.

97

Sentinel diesel locomotives return to the Loco Shed at Avonmouth Docks at the end of another working day during the summer of 1970.   The PBA internal rail fleet then numbered 23 engines and over 2000 wagons, mostly open rail trucks known as BDs.   In 1951, the first of the diesel locos arrived, and by 1965 the steam engines had been completely replaced.

A forest of West Wharf cranes.

Just an average day at the Eastern Arm during the 1970s: an Ellerman liner, the 7727-ton *City of Newcastle*, discharges animal feed produce at X Berth, a fleet of log-laden Ashmead barges await towage to the plywood factory at Lydney while, over at West Wharf, a Bank liner is kept busy. The nine-ton transporter crane relieves a coaster of its cargo – destination ICI Severnside; and around 20,000 tons of concentrates are transferred from bulk carrier by Kangaroo cranes to the Smelting Works' conveyor belt.

Eastern Arm activity – this Turkish vessel is towed towards the only available berth during a busy spell in the early-1970s. The Eastern Arm is a half-mile long and 400 feet wide. It can accommodate ten large ships, or quite a lot of smaller ones ...

Tea port ... throughout the 1970s Bristol was the premier port in the United Kingdom for the import of tea, handling over 40% of the nation's needs. Shipments arrived in conventional tea chests from Sri Lanka, Bangladesh, East Africa – and India.

Port puree ... flags were flown, bugles blown and a special ramp created at West Wharf 1 when Tarros Line introduced a regular roll on/roll off service with Salerno on 10 December, 1971. Tomato puree by the container load came ashore from the vessels employed on this Mediterranean run – *Vento di Maestrale* and *Vento di Scirocco*, both 1593 tons. The owners rented space in the port offices, but the imported puree dried up and the Italian team slipped quietly back to Salerno.

Cargo/passenger liner *Akaroa*, 18,565 tons, one of Shaw Savill's biggest ships in July 1971, is pictured at P Shed discharging 3000 tons of New Zealand meat just prior to being sold to a Greek shipping interest. The attractive little PBA tug *Cabot* was built in 1952 to replace the steam tug *Bulldog*. After chugging around the docks, shifting grain elevators and towing barges, she was sadly missed once sold to the Maritime Towing and Salvage Company for £30,000 in 1974.

The 30,000-ton capacity No 5 Granary, completed in 1966 and one of Bristol's tallest buildings, dominates this busy 1971 scene at the grain berths as Canadian wheat and barley are discharged overside to barge and coaster. Four public berths, with 2000 feet of quayage, were specially equipped to deal with the million tons of grain which came into port every year until the mid-1970s.

The high hopes of 1971, when this Ocean Container Terminal opened for business at T Shed, were soon dashed as the port waited in vain for container customers to use the new Strachan & Henshaw-built crane and other facilities. Three coasters did use the berth, but only because of a dock strike at their home port of Garston.

Traditional cranes gradually returned to the quayside late in 1972 and the big grey giant was shunted to the far end of T Shed to be used only by pigeons and the port photographer. It was quietly sold and shipped to Tasmania in the mid-1970s.

With dimensions of 875 feet by 100 feet, the Royal Edward Dry Dock is not only the largest in the Bristol Channel, but one of the biggest in the country. In April, 1972, the largest ship ever to drydock for repairs was the Indian m.v. *Chennai Jayam*, 24,355 tons and, despite its length of 667 feet, there was plenty of room to spare.

The narrowest section of the Royal Edward Dock is a 250-foot-wide branch at the south east corner which leads towards the Avonmouth Dock. 1972: to the left, a Polish vessel is discharging cargo at R Shed, while a consignment of refrigerated meat and dairy produce is off-loaded from the Federal liner *Westmorland* at the larger O Shed. The overhead conveyor system which connects the 1908-built shed to the Cold Stores can be observed at the bottom right.

A reel link ... one of the longest ships to use Avonmouth was the 683-foot *Laurentian Forest*, 16,380 tons, pictured in the locks en route for the newly constructed forest produce terminal with several thousand reels of newsprint. This new link with the Canadian ports, inaugurated on 24 November, 1972, was the largest dry cargo contract ever signed by the PBA. The largest newsprint carriers afloat, the *Laurentian Forest* and sister ship *Avon Forest* would make 24 round trips a year bringing newsprint to Britain and shipping cars to Canada. Two years later the Red Devils, as known to the dockers, transferred their affections and paper reels to Southampton.

Refrigerated liner *Sussex*, 11,272 tons, was one of several Federal Shipping Company vessels to lose their attractive livery and adopt the P & O colours in 1973. In January of that year, this 1949-built meat carrier broke all tonnage records after arriving in port with over 6000 tons of frozen produce from New Zealand.

On 5 April, 1973 the worst blaze for over twenty years occurred at W Shed when a cargo of jute ignited in No 3 hold of the Five Star liner *Mergui*, and spread rapidly to the bridge, accommodation and engine room.   Fast-thinking PBA foreman Mike Antill observed the early signs and called Bristol Fire Brigade.   The first of 12 fire engines arrived within fifteen minutes, but by then the 7458-ton Burmese vessel was well alight.   The crew had to evacuate ship leaving possessions behind, and were cared for by the Mission to Seamen in Portview Road. Fire fighters worked through the night and into the following day before ship repairers, Jefferies of Avonmouth, could board the water-logged mess, with an eleven degree list to starboard, to start making good the damage.

Bulk carrier *Finnish Wasa*, at 14,921 gross registered tons the largest ship to be registered in Bristol, came to West Wharf 5 during October, 1973 to discharge 25,000 tons of phosphate rock from Casablanca.   Built in 1966, this Swedish-owned vessel was leased to Whitwill Cole (Whitco Marine Services) and therefore was entitled to fly the red ensign and change the port of registry.

Evening draws in over the Royal Edward Dock ...

The imposing Shaw Savill liner *Ionic*, 10,987 tons, chugs slowly down the Eastern Arm towed by Cory's tug *Polgarth* just prior to sailing in December, 1973. The logs in the foreground had been discharged from the Ghanaian vessel *Offin River*, 7354 tons gross.

Kiwi pairing ... the 8181-ton *City of Auckland* and *Auckland Star*, 11,799 tons, meet up at the Royal Edward Dock during the summer of 1974.

Two at a time in 1974 ... no trouble for the largest dry dock in the Bristol Channel, and certainly no problem for the 300-strong workforce of Jefferies Ltd.   This graving dock, once a major asset to the Port, hasn't seen a ship for years.

1974 was a profitable year for petroleum imports with a total of 2 ½ million tons passing through the port's pipelines. The 630-foot *Texaco New Mexico*, 18,750 gross tons, was a typical example of tankers then using the Oil Basin.

C. J. King's tugs *Sea Volunteer* and *Sea Alert* manoeuvre the handsome Blue Star liner *Rockhampton Star*, 11,872 tons, towards the waiting dry dock for routine repairs before her voyage to Australia. A Shaw Savill bow can be seen in the foreground, while at the distant T Shed an Ellerman ship off-loads general cargo.

Men for all seasons – the lives of boatmen and tug crews are governed by tide timetables and shipping movements; and they frequently endure hostile weather, as do the Port's nautical staff, channel and dock pilots.

A seasonal shipment – every November a Chinese vessel would come to Avonmouth to discharge enough walnuts for everyone in the West Country to enjoy a Christmas feast.   The m.v. *Tian Shui*, 9333 grt, pictured at T Shed, managed to unload her 1000 tons of festive cargo just ahead of a fast looming storm on 19 November, 1975.

Kindred spirits – some of the Port's liquid assets, captured by the camera in the 1970s.

Fresh out of dry dock and ready to return to the English Channel is the 4011-ton ferry *Free Enterprise II* after being serviced and painted by Jefferies Ltd.   This was one of many cross-channel ferries that came for maintenance throughout the 1970s, speaking well for the skills of our ship repairers of the time.   Astern is Ellerman's general cargo liner, the 6919-ton *City of Gloucester*.

Inward bound ... the m.v. *Stadf Wolfsburg*, 15,434 tons, steers a course for No 3 Granary to discharge 18,000 tons of barley during May, 1975.

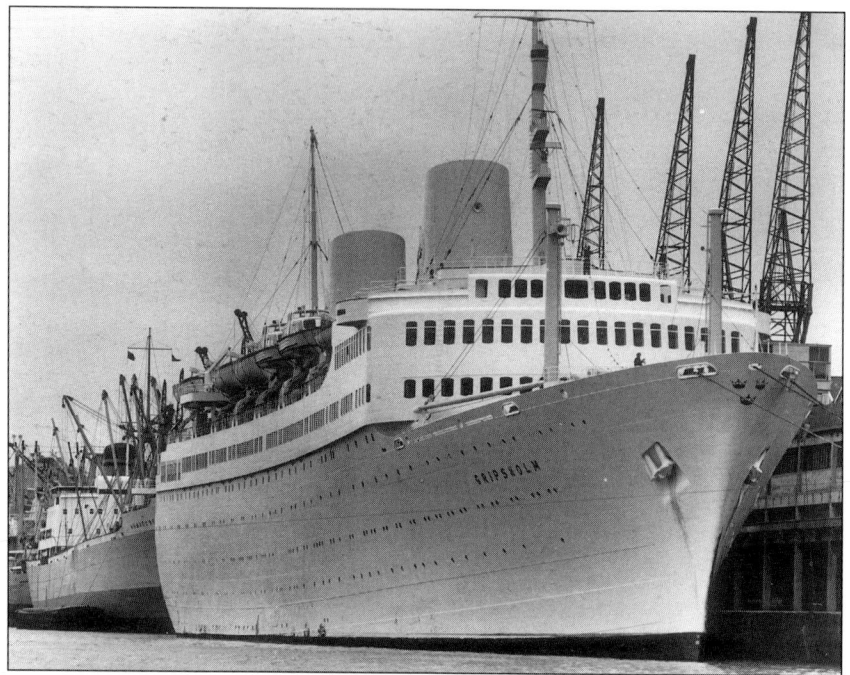

Replacing the mv. *Kungsholm* for one cruise around the UK in June, 1975 was the Swedish-American luxury liner *Gripsholm*, 22,557 tons, and she looked an impressive sight berthed at V Shed in the Royal Edward Dock. Her larger sister *Kungsholm* became, at 26,678 tons, the biggest ship to enter the Port of Bristol on 16 May, 1972, although her overall dimensions were slightly smaller than the m.v. *Chennai Ookham*'s which previously held the record at 24,365 gross registered tons.

Hardwood logs from West Africa were discharged from this 7446-ton Ghanaian vessel by ship's derrick to Ashmead's barges at X Berth during the summer of 1975, while the tug *Peter Leigh* ensured a steady supply of barges. Around this time, 30,000 tons of this cumbersome cargo were shipped into Avonmouth each year, loaded to barge and then towed to Factories Direct Ltd at Lydney – the largest veneer and plywood mill in Great Britain. Ashmead's tug *Peter Leigh* was previously the well known river tug *John King*. Astern of the *Nakwa River* is an Indian liner discharging tea at W Shed.

Piped ashore ... a 12,770-grt Liberian-registered tanker at the Oil Basin in 1975.

C. J. King's tugs *Sea Bristolian* and *Sea Volunteer* take the stern ropes as a large bulk timber carrier prepares to sail from S Shed in the winter of 1975.

Juicy Jaffas – all 65,000 boxes of them are cheerfully discharged from the m.v. *Maranga* by happy Bristol dockers at S Shed on 29 January, 1976.

While petroleum is spirited ashore from the 17,892-ton *Texaco Kentucky*, her neighbour *Joseph P. Grace*, 9942 gross tons, pumps a tank of gas into port pipelines during 1975.

Bananas – the first shipment in nine years – were, after a ceremony at S Shed attended by local luminaries, port people and the press, discharged from the Fyffes Group liner *Tucurina*, 6712 tons, during March, 1976. The occasion marked the 75th anniversary of the first shipment of the fruit into Bristol when on 18 March, 1901, the 2830-ton steamer *Port Morant* brought 18,000 stems from Jamaica.

P & O ... plenty and often!   So it seemed for a few years after 1973, when the Federal Steam Navigation fleet was changed to P & O colours.   Here, on 10 June, 1976, two arrived at the same time – the 7602 ton *Somerset* was first through the locks, with the 10,792-ton cadet ship *Otaio* coming between the piers before entering the port.   Both liners berthed at P & O Sheds in the Royal Edward Dock and discharged frozen lamb which contributed to the 82,000 tons of New Zealand meat imported through Bristol that year.

Shipping movements during the summer of 1976.

This aerial view of the Royal Edward Dock in 1976 shows (bottom right) a vessel passing through the 1877 locks into the Avonmouth Dock a few months before this port entrance was closed on 14 November. What remains of the East and West Piers can also be seen, plus a section of the BOCM Mill – long since gone. The Oil Basin, tank farms and Eastern Arm are visible at the top left, north of the turning basin.

General view of the Eastern Arm in 1976.

Loaded to the mark with African goods, the m.v. *Benefactor*, 11,299 tons – the largest of Harrison Line's general cargo ships – is towed through the Royal Edward locks by King's tug *Sea Merrimac* during the hot summer of 1976. Originally Greek-owned and named *Ion*, the *Benefactor* was one of 29 ships flying the Harrison flag at that time.

Lower easy ... African logs come ashore from the Elder Dempster liner *Stentor* in 1976. This handsome, 1946 rivet-built ship of 9833 tons originally belonged to Alfred Holt's Blue Funnel fleet.

This nine-ton transporter crane, used primarily for ICI bulk imports, dominated the West Wharf for twenty-five years until it was dismantled in the late-1980s. Pictured is the 3057-ton Icelandic vessel *Hvalvik*, discharging 4100 tons of phosphate rock from Dakar, West Africa, in September, 1976.

Outside the Royal Edward locks waits a Russian ship anxious to enter port while within the turning basin the Elder Dempster liner *Falaba*, 7703 tons, on the inaugural voyage of a new West African Express Service, is being manoeuvred into her berth at S Shed.

Ellerman's *City of Lichfield*, 7012 tons, reflects on her beauty while discharging a cargo of tea from India at X berth during November, 1976.

Busy, busy, busy ...

This 7827-ton Nigerian liner discharged a full cargo of cocoa beans at X berth in 1977 – a significant contribution to the 30,000 tons handled at the port that year.

The m.v. *Indian Trust*, 9975 tons, pictured in 1977 discharging bales of cotton, was one of a fleet of fine-looking ships belonging to the India Steam Ship Company, frequent visitors to the Port of Bristol.

118

Long way round ... with the closure of the Avonmouth Old Locks in November, 1976, ships left or entered the Old Dock by way of the Royal Edward Dock and the 85-foot wide inter-connecting Junction Cut. Bristol Seaways' 1241-ton *Echo* does just that as she glides past the Bangladeshi liner *Banglar Swapna*, 6851 tons, berthed at R Shed, and P & O's *Westmorland*, 8230 tons, at O Shed, during the summer of 1977. The 1906 swing bridge in the foreground was converted to scrap metal in 1992.

Union Castle liner *Balmoral Castle*, 7952 tons – formerly *Clan Robertson* – discharges general cargo from South Africa at P Shed while a Simca car, part of a shipment of used vehicles, is lowered into a hold at S Shed for export to Colombo in December, 1977.

Worldwide trading – the Pacific Steam Navigation vessel *Ortega*, 12,321 tons, arrives from South America with containers and general cargo as dockers off-load a consignment of Far Eastern lumber while, in the background, a Blue Star liner discharges Australian cheese and apples during August, 1978.

Sailings and arrivals ... a little traffic builds up around the port entrance as a Harrison liner clears the locks making way for a couple of general cargo ships to enter the docks during summer, 1979.   King's 102 feet-long *Sea Challenge* came into service on 12 January, 1968 to replace the lovely steam tug *Bristolian*, which towed thousands of ships safely into port during her fifty-six years' service.

Harrison liner *Craftsman*, 10,219 tons, equipped with jumbo derricks capable of lifting 500 tons, passes the world's largest refrigerated vessel *Port Chalmers*, 16,283 tons, as she prepares to leave port in May, 1979.

C. J. King's tugs race out to the Port approaches during May, 1979, anxious to tow the oncoming vessels safely into harbour.

Passing the North Pier – this 8,152-ton Polish liner gets a tow into Royal Edward Dock, while the French vessel *Mansart*, 16,649 tons, has to wait her turn to enter port on 31 May, 1979.

We have the cranes – just send us the ships ...

Over 4000 tons of gas oil are transferred from Unitank's storage tanks to this 4467-ton French carrier for export to Rotterdam during October, 1981.

The end of the line ... a great chapter of British shipping history ended on 1 October, 1981 when the very last Clan liner afloat arrived at the Royal Edward Dock from India with a cargo of tea and some manhole covers.   After discharge, *Clan MacGregor*, 8811 tons, sailed to Manchester to be sold, so ending 103 years of trading history and a long association with the Port of Bristol.

Hands up! Publicity officer Rodney Stone and a Geest long-haul truck driver were delighted to see Bristol back in the banana business.   The Geest Line, after many years of trading between Barry Dock and the Windward Islands, switched to Avonmouth and on 29 November, 1981, the m.v. *Geestbay*, 7,729 tons, arrived at O Shed with the first shipment.

The new business provided employment and breathed life back into O and P Sheds, under-used for many months since the cessation of the meat trade with New Zealand.
But sadly this banana re-birth was short-lived.   Only twenty-seven months later, after industrial unrest and acrimonious exchanges, Geest returned to South Wales in February, 1984.

Geestport, the 7729-ton flagship of the Geest banana fleet, enters the Royal Edward Dry Dock for a good clean-up and overhaul on 24 August, 1982, after serving as a Task Force supply ship in the Falklands war.

The m.v. *Frisian Explorer*, 3986 tons, loads cement during May, 1986 for the last of 35 voyages to the Falkland Islands.   Following the 1982 war, Bristol was chosen to ship out machinery, materials and supplies to improve the airport and other sections for the future defence of the islands.   From September, 1983 to May, 1986, the Cenargo Shipping Company delivered over 700,000 tons of cargo to the South Atlantic.

The port tried to grab all it could in the lean 1980s.

A busy period like this in 1986 was a welcome relief.

Grain era crumbles ... the golden days were over for No 3 Granary when, during June 1988, a demolition squad was turned loose on this imposing waterfront landmark.   A few months later, the sixty-year old structure was no more.   In February, 1989, dust was replaced by rust when the Bird Group acquired the berth to export scrap metal.

Concrete proposals ... it was good news for Bristol Docks when Castle Cement agreed to use X berth in the Eastern Arm as their bulk import terminal and to utilise the redundant Fison storage tanks. Although there was still a little work to complete at the berth, the 8115-ton *Furunes* arrived with the first shipment of cement on 6 May, 1989 ... and it has been plain sailing ever since.

Heavy metal ... where once a mighty granary stood, scrap metal now resides. After demolition of No 3 Granary, Allied Bird Fragmentation installed a 20-ton crane, and soon established themselves as the largest scrap metal exporters in Europe. This 13,993-ton Malaysian bulk carrier, *Rimba Balau*, was the fifteenth ship to use the berth when she loaded a record cargo in September, 1989.

End of the trail ... the RMS *St Helena* takes on board cargo and passengers for the last time at O Shed on 7 July, 1990.   After twelve years of regular sailings between Bristol and the South Atlantic islands of Ascension and St Helena, this 3150-ton vessel was replaced by a larger ship of the same name.   Andrew Bell, manager of the St Helena Shipping Company, had hoped to continue operating from Bristol, but the tide ran against him, and the new ship now sets forth from Cardiff on its fifty-three-day round voyage.

Royal Portbury Dock

Giant parking lot ... this was how the Royal Portbury waterfront looked in 1983 – and they are still spilling onto the quayside at over 200,000 a year ...

[overleaf] Bridge-high with boxes, the Singapore-registered *TFL Express*, 13,941 tons, was part of a regular, twice-monthly, sailing schedule between Bristol and Halifax, Nova Scotia, during the early-1980s.   For a while, Royal Portbury Dock was the sole port of call for the continent and the UK in this important North American trade link.

Bristol's ambitions for a dock worthy of the twenty-first century were translated into reality on 8 August, 1977 when Her Majesty the Queen, accompanied by Prince Philip, formally opened the West Dock and, by so doing, changed its name to Royal Portbury Dock.

The royal couple had arrived in the royal yacht *Britannia* and, after being piped ashore, were received by the Lord Lieutenant, Sir John Wills, who escorted them to the ceremonial dais at No 2 berth. Bristol's Lord Mayor, Councillor Ted Wright, drew the loudest cheer of the day when he announced that this was a dock for Bristol – and paid for by Bristolians. There would be no government grant.

Bristol now had the dock, it had the men, but it would have to wait another eight months to sight its first ship.

The Portbury story could be said to date from 1958 when Bristol Corporation bought a large parcel of land, bounded by the Avon on one side and the Pill to Portishead railway line on the other. The possibilities of dock expansion across the Portbury marshes had occupied the minds of the Port Authority for some time and when, in 1962, the Rochdale Committee enquiring into Britain's major ports revealed there were more deep-water berths in Antwerp than in the whole of Great Britain, the Bristol Docks Committee decided to build a new dock at Portbury.

The Royal Edward Dock would eventually be unable to accommodate the larger bulk carriers and container vessels which, the trends were indicating, would soon dominate the ocean trade routes. Bristol history repeated itself for the seventh time in 150 years as port expansionists were yet again crying for a larger lock entrance. The desire for a new super dock was not, unfortunately, coupled with the opportunity to build it; and the 1960s proved a decade of intense frustration.

In May 1964 an impressive plan for a dock basin with three large extension arms offering over 30 deep-water berths for giant tankers and bulkers was submitted to the Ministry of Transport. The estimated cost was £27 million. After an anxious two-year wait, the scheme was rejected in July 1966 on the grounds that it was too ambitious. Another plan for a smaller scheme costing £15 million was submitted the following year, and again turned down.

Undaunted, the Docks Committee submitted an alternative, £13.8 million proposal in March, 1970. Another long wait was anticipated, but three months later a general election returned a new government to Westminster and with it fresh hopes for Bristol's new dock. The Conservative Minister for Transport Industries, John Peyton, was approached and gave his consent in November of that year. The final hurdle was cleared on 1 July, 1971 with the House of Commons voting 128 to 18 in favour of the proposal. Bristol's jubilation was, however, tempered with the announcement that no government aid would be forthcoming.

The West Dock would now be financed through the Corporation's consolidated loan fund; the Docks would borrow from it, and pay interest at the prevailing rate. But the seven-year delay in obtaining governmental go-ahead had cost Bristol dearly. Through the 1960s rival ports had been developing container and bulk terminal facilities while Bristol's new dock remained pinned to the drawing board. On 2 May, 1972 – a full ten years after the Docks Committee's decision to dig the Portbury marshes and meadows – John Peyton drove the first sheet piles to start the scheme. By September, 1975 the hole in the ground had become the West Dock, with its concrete quays in place.

The dock basin is quadrilateral in shape with a water area of 70 acres to a depth of 45 feet. Continuous quays 2000 feet long are provided on three sides, offering a total wharfage of 6000 feet. The locks, the largest in the United Kingdom, are 1200 feet long by 140 feet wide – almost eight times greater than the Cumberland Basin entrance into the City Docks. The Gordano Quay, consisting of berths 1 and 2, was the first section to be developed and included a forest produce warehouse, offices and a 40-ton container crane.

Gearbulk Ltd, the Norwegian bulk carriers, had promised to use the dock and on 12 April, 1978 the company's *Kiwi Arrow*, 24,999 tons gross, was the first customer through the locks, bringing 8000 tons of forest produce. It was an exciting start and a confidence-booster to operations managers John Churches and Bernard Pepworth.

Shipping input during the early months was slow, but the following year Royal Portbury was well established as a container dock and with so many shipments arriving the Docks Committee decided to order another giant container crane to cope with the increased traffic. This was assembled on berth and operational early in 1982. The import of cars began to grow, with Abbey Hill developing 25 acres of hard standing. In January, 1982 United Molasses set up a new storage and distribution plant at Portbury, leaving the premises they had occupied for many years at Avonmouth Dock.

Portbury seemed to be thriving, but overall the Port of Bristol was in bad financial shape, owing in part to the loss of many liner trades at Avonmouth, and in particular to crippling interest payments levied on the £34 million capital cost of Royal Portbury Dock. In 1986 the container trade dwindled dramatically and over the next four years the twin container cranes were so under-employed that they were sold and shipped to the Middle East.

It wasn't all gloom: Redland Plasterboard opened a factory just outside the dock to import gypsum via a conveyor system linked to No 4 berth on St George's Quay. More and more automobiles occupied the newly-paved berths 3 and 4, while the forest produce tonnage continued to increase at berths 1 and 2.

Two berths on the River Quay, however, remained undeveloped which meant that, at its busiest time, the dock could realise only two-thirds of its potential earning power. Despite a favourable restructuring of the Port's finances in 1986 – along with a gradual upsurge in trade as the decade drifted into 1990 – major capital investment was required to develop fully all berths at Royal Portbury Dock. The City Council did not have the resources, and decided on 22 August, 1991 to lease the Port of Bristol to a commercial operator, First Corporate Shipping Ltd.

The chairman of the Docks Committee, Councillor Doug Naysmith explained the dilemma facing the council: 'It is a pity that at this stage the port is to leave the City Council's control, but I believe there is really no alternative. Without the investment that First Corporate has pledged to provide, surviving in the current competitive ports industry would be far from certain.'

It was a courageous decision of great historical importance, and hindsight shows it to have been the correct one. All credit, though, must go to those members of the Bristol Docks Committee who fought against government indifference so vigorously throughout the 1960s. Their sense of determination and enterprise places them alongside the great Bristol visionaries of the nineteenth century. Without a Royal Portbury Dock and the focus of attention and trade on Europe, Bristol would indeed be very much a fifth-rate maritime force today.

Optimistic view ... had Bristol been allowed to build its West Dock in the 1960s, Royal Portbury might well have looked like this imaginative impression created by Clifford Ashley in 1964.

At last! On 2 May, 1972 the Rt Hon. John Peyton, Minister for Transport and Industry, breaks new ground by sinking a sheet pile deep into Portbury soil. The project engineer William Sivewright and chairman Cllr Ted Wright look happy – the contractors at either side are more restrained, no doubt contemplating five years' toil ahead of them ...

Taking shape ... on 2 May, 1974 – exactly two years after the official West Dock go-ahead ceremony – the Portbury meadows and marshes were being transformed into a 50-foot deep, 70-acre hole in the ground. The construction of the entrance lock, top of picture, is well under way. Sixteen months later, it was filled with water and Bristol's dreams for a dock worthy of the twenty-first century gradually became reality.

Not long now ... the water was in the dock and the mighty 1200 feet by 140 feet locks, in this March, 1977 aerial view, were already opened to the trade routes of the world.

Went the day well ... the royal yacht *Britannia* and her escort HMS *Fife* sail through the locks and into the night – twelve hours after HM The Queen officially opened the Royal Portbury Dock. It was a great day for the port and a major history-making occasion for Bristol.

Ready to go ... the workforce chosen to operate the new Royal Portbury Dock, under the leadership of John Churches and Bernard Pepworth, pose for the camera in 1978.

Open for business at last ... on 12 April, 1978, six years after the ground-breaking ceremony, Royal Portbury Dock receives its first customer, the m.v. *Kiwi Arrow* with 8000 tons of plywood and pulp from British Columbia. Several small craft had entered the new dock since it was flooded on 4 September, 1975, but this 24,999-ton Gearbulker was the real history-maker.

The Swedish-American cruise liner *Kungsholm*, 26,678 tons, brings 450 passengers into the newly opened Royal Portbury Dock in May, 1978, as part of a thirty-seven-day tour of the British Isles. Despite entering the Royal Edward Dock without incident in previous years, this 87-feet beam by 666-feet long vessel appears to be experiencing some difficulty negotiating the much larger Royal Portbury lock entrance.

This was her last visit to the Bristol Channel; following this cruise, this magnificent ship was acquired by the P & O Group and renamed *Sea Princess*.

Swing it boys ... the 26,844-ton *Seatrain Rotterdam* arrives at Royal Portbury on her maiden voyage in August, 1978, to discharge 106 containers from Rotterdam and load 142 for shipment to the Middle East.
Right – hobblers struggle to make her fast.

New horizons opened up on 22 July, 1979 when the Trans-Freight liner *Visurgis*, 5997 tons, arrived at Portbury to establish a container link between the UK and the South-eastern Seaboard – a service eventually extended to Halifax, Nova Scotia.

French connection ... an attractive visitor to Gordano Quay was the Le Havre-registered *Fort Royal*, 32,671 tons, pictured loading containers for North America on 28 August, 1979.

Sisters ... Gearbulk twins *Strinda*, 24,997 gross tons, and *Kiwi Arrow*, 24,999 tons, get together in the south corner of Royal Portbury Dock during the summer of 1979. The Gearbulk carrier enterprise was founded in the late-1960s by Kristian Gerard Jebsen in Bergen, Norway, and has since developed into a powerful consortium.

The ships have five box-shaped holds with no overhangs, obstructions or tween-decks – the bulk facility. The gear part is offered by the distinctive gantry cranes mounted on the ships' decks. The first Gearbulker into Bristol was the m.v. *Heina* which arrived at the Royal Edward Dock with Canadian forest produce at Easter, 1976. In 1979, Gearbulk brought 390,000 tons of cargo to the port.

Exciting times – only sixteen months after the first cargo arrived at Royal Portbury, three seems a crowd as Norwegian, French and Spanish vessels occupy berths 1, 2 and 3 in August, 1979.

Bountiful boxes ... within two years of its official opening, Royal Portbury was playing host to giant container vessels like the 52,444-ton *Ortelius*, pictured on 2 December, 1979.   It was lucrative business while it lasted – which wasn't long enough.

A mariner's view of the largest locks in the U.K. as the Scan Carrier m.v. *Tourcoing*, 22,435 tons, enters Royal Portbury Dock in April 1980 with a shipload of containers from Bordeaux.

Happy mix ... Mitsubishi cars and Massey Ferguson tractors meet on the Gordano Quay waterfront during the summer of 1980.   Within two years of trading, the potential of Royal Portbury's vast acreage was fully realised.

The 600-foot long *La Ensenada*, 25,532 grt, prepares to berth at Gordano Quay with 18,800 tons of forest produce during August, 1980.

Ships that pass in the night ... Span Line's *Esther Del Mar*, 1997 tons, loads containers for Bilbao as another container vessel slips her moorings and heads for the locks to catch the late-evening tide during December, 1980.

Keep those Fergies moving – Bristol dockers make short work of loading a consignment of 1145 British-built Massey Ferguson tractors aboard the 8403-ton *Garnet Ace* in June, 1981. They were bound for the Middle East.

The m.v. *Osaka Bay*, 58,889 tons gross, held the record for twelve years as the largest ship to enter the Port of Bristol, after docking on 28 November, 1981 with a cargo of 654 containers from Japan. Despite being beaten on tonnage, the *Osaka Bay*, at 950 feet, remains the longest ship to use the port.

Keep heaving ... three determined Cory tugs work hard to dock the fully-laden Gearbulker *La Sierra*, 28,004 registered tons, alongside Gordano Quay in spring, 1982.

How things change ... this 1982 view of Royal Portbury Dock is altogether different today: gone are the two container cranes at Gordano Quay ... gone is the distant Portishead power station ... gone are acres of waste ground, now committed to concrete as hard-standing for cars and forest produce – and now, completely dominating the River Quay in the foreground, stands a huge animal feed terminal ... what a difference a decade makes.

All fired up with somewhere to go ... Cory tugs *Pengarth* and *Point Gilbert* are anxious to get out to King Road as they steam out of the Portbury locks in the summer of 1982. About to leave port, at a more leisurely pace, is the 25,223 grt *Alain L. D.*

Bulk carriers *Angelic Grace*, 30,193 tons gross, and *Angelic Protector*, 34,130 tons, pictured at Portbury in October, 1982, were two of six bulkers laid up for long periods during the early 1980s. Their presence enhanced the atmosphere of the dock, making it appear busy during quiet times, and also provided the Port Authority with additional revenue.

Treacle treat ... the 17,485-ton *Mathraki* – the very first tanker to use Royal Portbury Dock – is seen arriving at St George's Quay in December, 1982 with 25,000 tons of molasses destined for the newly located United Molasses distribution centre, whose storage tanks are on the right.   Also, just visible, are tanks belonging to the old depot across the river at Avonmouth which was phased out in the spring of 1983.

Cars, containers and Canadian lumber – all part of the Portbury scene in the 1980s.

The impressive 100-foot beam by 660 feet long m.v. *Beltimber*, 27,470 tons gross, comes alongside Gordano Quay in October, 1986 with a cargo of 102 containers and 5000 tons of Canadian lumber.

Heading for shore – the first Honda cars arrive at St George's Quay in 1986.

The shape of ships to come ... not very elegant, but delivering the goods. This 15,939-ton vehicle carrier brought 1931 Nissan cars to Portbury compounds on her maiden voyage from Japan in May, 1987. Custom-built for the automobile trade, the *Honmoku Maru* can carry over 5000 cars in 12 decks.

Redland Plasterboard displayed confidence in Royal Portbury Dock by investing £25 million in a new factory, linked to quay wall facilities by an overhead gantry conveyor system. In September, 1989 the first shipment of 35,000 tons of rock gypsum from Spain arrived aboard the 23,955-ton *Atlantic Superior*. Since then, imports of gypsum – used in the manufacture of plasterboard – have averaged 250,000 tons annually. This could well double beyond the mid-1990s, as Redland have embarked on a further £20 million expansion programme at their 9-acre site.

Sorry to see you go ... a lone port worker watches the 5496-ton *Dock Express 12* carry away the two container cranes from Royal Portbury Dock on 1 August, 1990. It took two days to load this pair of 700-ton Titans which, following the dramatic decline in container trade, had been under-used since 1986. They were sold to Eurolift Plant and shipped to Sharjah, in the United Arab Emirates.

Out you go ... the Panamanian car carrier *Seijin*, 15,397 tons, gets nudged out of port by Cory King tug *Point James* after discharging vehicles in 1991.

The Bristol Port Company:
the Docks since 1991

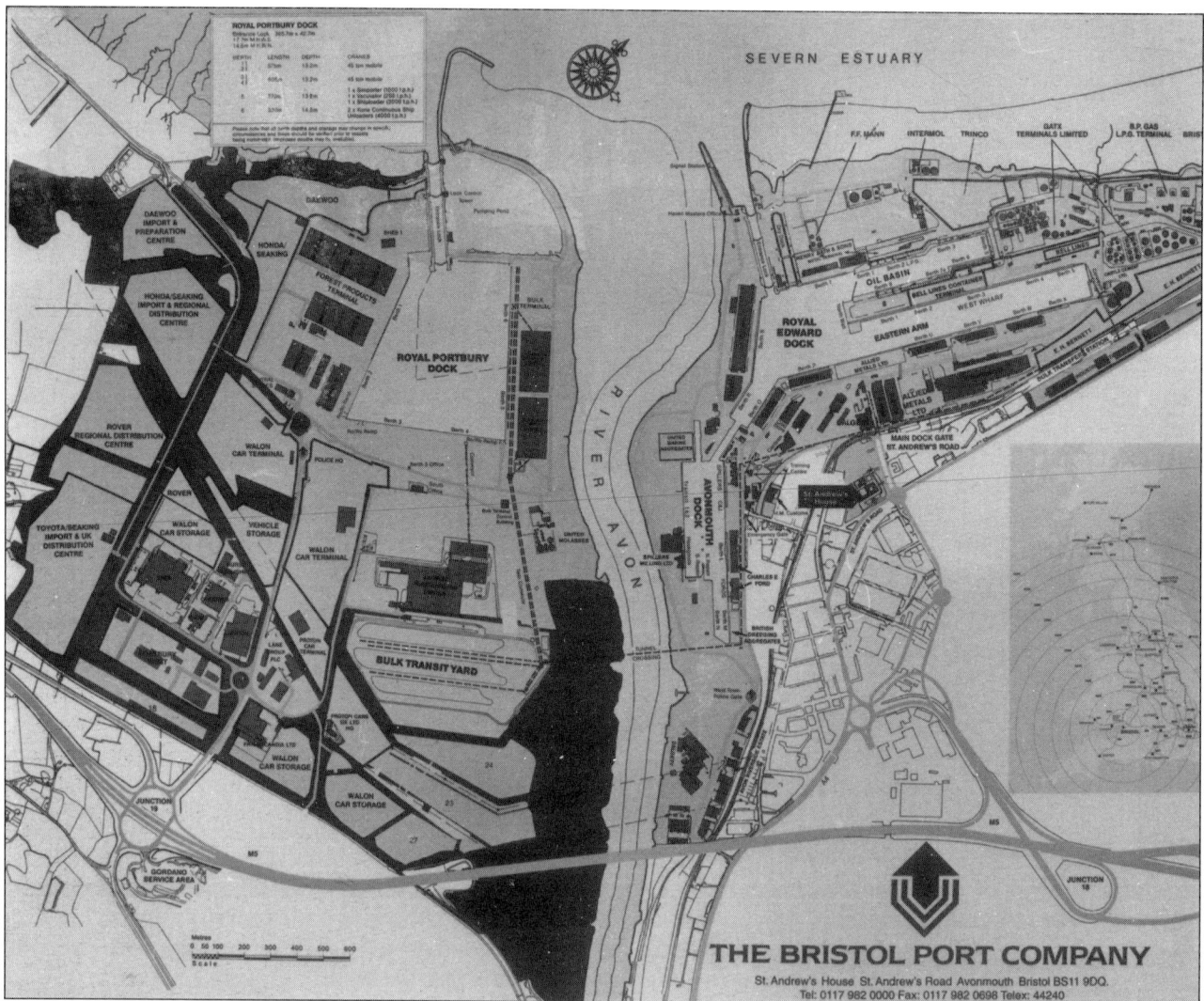

The modern Port of Bristol, located on both banks at the mouth of the River Avon, covers a land and water area of four square miles.

(*overleaf*) Trading trends of the 1990s ... giant bulk carriers like the *Captain Veniamis*, pictured arriving at Royal Portbury Dock with 100,000 tons of animal feed, are now frequent visitors to the modern Port of Bristol.

Before the sun had chance to set over the yard arm on 27 August, 1991, Bristol had become a born-again port. Helmed by Terence Mordaunt and David Ord, the Bristol Port Company – newly formed out of First Corporate Shipping – had set a course towards a bright and prosperous horizon. It was a day that marked the end of 143 years of control by the City Council – Bristol Docks were now in private hands, and the colours and logos of the sixty-five-year old Port of Bristol Authority gave way to new corporate images.

The Port Authority had struggled through, and survived, the gloomy, trade-depressed 1980s – a period when several British ports foundered and, by 1981, with the exception of Tilbury in Essex, all the London docks had closed, including the mighty Royal group. Bristol, on the other hand, had resolutely refused to give in. And, as the hungry 1980s made way for the 1990s, the Port sailed into the new decade in a more buoyant mood with a restructured and flexible workforce – tonnages were up, morale was higher, and the future looked altogether brighter ...

To maintain this momentum, capital investment would be needed to cater for modern trading trends without which the port's new-found zeal would founder. But with central government restrictions on council borrowing, Bristol could offer nothing but hope. The arrival of First Corporate Shipping was timely. Company chairman Terence Mordaunt and managing director David Ord had for some time harboured an ambition to run their own port and, by early 1990, had set their sights on Bristol. They submitted an offer, issuing a press statement on 2 October, 1990:

> Our objective is straightforward. We aim to create a thriving enterprise at the
> Avonmouth and Portbury docks for the continuing benefit of all those who
> depend upon the Port of Bristol for their jobs and their business. We believe
> that a modern, commercially viable port is vital to the prosperity of Bristol and
> we are convinced that this goal is achievable.

To the surprise of some and the disbelief of others, the City Council took the company's offer seriously. The transformation in the port's fortunes in the past five years suggests that history will record their decision as a wise and momentous one.

There's a ship coming in ... all 60,551 tons of this bulk carrier bear down on the Royal Portbury entrance lock on 22 June, 1993 – bringing with it some 37,000 tons of coal from the U.S.A.   This was the largest vessel to date to use the dock, and her 133-foot beam allowed little room for manoeuvre in the 140-feet wide entrance.

This general view of Royal Portbury Dock in November, 1993 shows forest produce vessels berthed at Gordano Quay, with car carriers occupying berths 3 and 4 of the St George's Quay to the right.   Across the dock the first stage of the 200,000-ton bulk storage facility is operational at the River Quay with the Kone continuous discharge cranes in place.   A year later, the second storage section was completed and – after fifteen years of undeveloped idleness – berths 5 and 6 were finally open for business.

Ringing the changes ... just one of the 50,000 containers Bell Line plan to ship every year between Bristol, Spain and Ireland, from their £3 $\frac{1}{2}$ million terminal which opened late-November, 1993, dramatically changing the appearance of West Wharf.

One of the great achievements at Royal Portbury in the early-1990s was the installation of bulk terminal facilities at berths 5 and 6 which, before, had remained bereft of investment and development since the dock opened in 1977.   Enjoying the benefits of modern discharge methods along the 2000 feet of quay are 63,146-ton Russian bulker *Akademik Sechenov* and the 39,306-ton Norwegian carrier *Acina*.

Looming large – not the largest ship to travel through the UK's biggest lock, but with a beam of 133 feet and four inches, the Greek-registered, 60,846-ton *Captain Veniamis* certainly looked impressive on arrival at Portbury in August, 1994 with 100,000 tons of bulk animal feed.

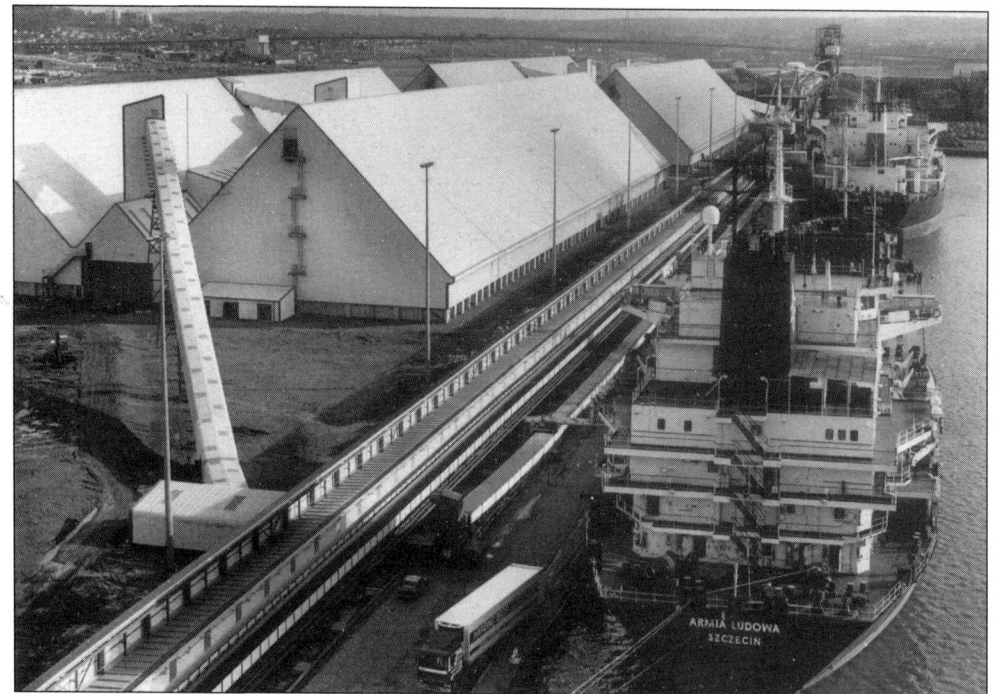

Two bulk carriers prepare to discharge cargoes of animal feed stuffs at the Agricultural Bulk Services' 200,000-ton capacity terminal, alongside Portbury's berths 5 and 6 in February, 1995. The once barren section of quay had remained undeveloped since it opened in 1977. Sixteen years on, this computerized storage facility – the most sophisticated in Great Britain – was created in a joint venture between the Bristol Port Company and Tate & Lyle.

Over one million tons of bulk animal feed came into the Bristol docks during 1994; as this trade is gradually switched from Royal Edward Dock, extra storage space will be needed at Portbury, where large bulk cargo ships with draughts up to 45 feet can easily be accommodated.

154

The fun starts here – favoured by West Country passengers and tour operators, Bristol has established a good reputation as an embarkation port for short-haul sea cruises to sun spots around the Spanish and North African coastlines. The 17,042-ton cruise liner *Southern Cross*, seen coming alongside No 4 berth, was one of many passenger ships to enjoy the spacious facilities at Royal Portbury Dock throughout the summer of 1995.

Great ships like this 63,649-ton, Panamanian-registered bulker, m.v. *Loussio*, with a beam of 134 feet, have become commonplace at Portbury since a modern bulk cargo terminal was developed in the early 1990s. The giant Kone continuous unloaders, seen here in September, 1995, are capable of discharging around 2000 tons of bulk commodities an hour.

Trades, tried and trusted ... the 18,960-ton, Limassol-registered m.v. *Flecha* discharges a large shipment of hardwoods from the Far East at S Shed for the Denholm Shipping Company while, just clearing the locks, the 2130-ton *Corinna* steers a course for the Bell Line container terminal at Royal Edward's West Wharf 3 in September, 1995.

Car quays – the Port of Bristol is now the largest importer of cars into the U.K. with around $^1/_4$ million vehicles shipped annually through Royal Portbury.   These two auto carriers at No 3 berth in October, 1995 are typical of the vessels which import and export motor cars in vast quantities from such manufacturers as Toyota, Daewoo, Honda, Rover, Vauxhall, Fiat, Alfa Romeo, Proton, Mitsubishi and Ford.

Broad in the beam ... with a width of 136 ¹/₂ feet, this 63,240-grt P & O bulk carrier was, on 6 November, 1995, the widest ship ever to enter the enclosed waters of the Port of Bristol. Allowing a gap only 21 inches on either side of her 873-foot hull, and drawing 46 feet of water, the m.v. *Duhallow* passed, without incident, through the Royal Portbury entrance lock like a dog through a hoop. Her cargo of 107,000 tons of coal from Baltimore took only 3 ¹/₂ days to discharge via two Kone continuous bulk cargo cranes which are linked to an extensive conveyor belt system direct to the rail head at Avonmouth.

Coal delivery ... this 23,909-ton bulk carrier had to dock at the top of the tide when she arrived at Royal Edward Dock's West Wharf in November, 1995, with 37 $\frac{1}{2}$ feet of her hull below the waterline.   The cargo of 36,867 tons of coal was discharged direct from the ship into bulk cargo lorries and transported to the adjacent E. H. Bennett distribution centre with the minimum of fuss or dust.

Diverse shipments ... a cargo of gypsum from Spain is discharged from the 14,387-ton Norwegian freighter *Wani Swan* at Portbury's No 4 berth and conveyed several hundred yards along an overhead system to the Lafarge Plasterboard works during 14 November, 1995.   Across the water at No 6 berth, the 64,475-ton Greek bulk carrier *Flag Mersindi* is relieved of a shipment of Louisiana cattle feed by Kone cranes which transport it, via a conveyor-belt network, directly into the Agricultural Bulk Services terminal.

New year joy. 1996 started well for the Bristol Port Company with the arrival of a new customer on 7 January – the 39,535-ton Wilhelmsen liner *Toba*. The Norwegian-owned line is the biggest roll on/roll off operator in the world and highly regarded in international shipping circles. This shipment – the first of a twice-monthly service – brought 8500 tons of woodpulp from Canada and, despite a towage system unfamiliar to the work-force, was discharged two hours ahead of schedule.

Wilhelmsen Lines had decided, in September, 1995, to switch its operations from Tilbury to Bristol. Modern warehouse facilities have since been constructed at Portbury along with the purchase of specialized handling equipment to cope with this trade. And – as with every type of commodity handled at Bristol's waterfront – an extensive training programme has been set in motion to ensure that port operatives deliver the goods swiftly, successfully and, above all, safely.

In you come, my babby…the 60,551 grt *Pytchley* presented few problems for the Port's nautical staff as her 870' x 133' bulk sailed gracefully into Royal Portbury's enormous entrance lock on 22 June, 1993.

How we have grown!   This 1996 aerial view of Royal Portbury Dock clearly shows the rapid developments since the Bristol Port Company took over in autumn, 1991.   The 70-acre dock basin that loomed so large when it first opened in the late 1970s seems now to be dwarfed when set against the vast acreage of activity which surrounds it.

Port-pourri

Ashmead's tug *Thelm Leigh* being raised on 16 January, 1978 after sinking in the Old Dock on Christmas Day when she was squeezed by one of F. T. Everard's ships at Hosegood's berth.   Formerly the British Waterways tug *Resolute*, she was restored to her original beauty by a gentleman from Westbury-on-Severn, renamed *Resolute Lady* and was kept busy during 1993 working for the contractors constructing the new Severn Bridge.

(overleaf) Royal highlight ... in 1973, Bristol celebrated the 600th anniversary of its county status.   On 9 August, H.M. The Queen added greatly to the festivities by spending a day in the city and the port was honoured by the arrival of the royal yacht *Britannia*, accompanied by HMS *Bristol*.   The photograph shows Her Majesty at the North Wall, escorted by the Lord Mayor, Cllr Wally Jenkins, with Mr and Mrs Gordon Lowery watching in the background.

In the day-to-day life of a busy port many interesting things happen outside the main business of loading and unloading ships. Royal visits, ministerial outings, ground-breaking events, history book happenings, civic ceremonies and social and sporting occasions – all serve to add colour and interest.

The dockers, for their part, made the day swing along with their down-to-earth and quirky humour, coining nicknames for one another – Pig's Ear, Bent Nose, Turkey Neck, Sponge Head, Chair Legs, Apple Face, Rubber Duck, Powder Puff, Cat Strangler, Angry Dwarf, Dolly Eyes, Rigor Mortis, 12-Volt, Rat Catcher, Hollywood Docker, Jumping Jack, Yogi Bear, Still Life, and a hundred more ... These were the days of the 'black books' and hooks.   Even the honourable appellation 'docker' has disappeared – all are port operatives in these more sophisticated days.

This final selection of photographs reflects this pot-pourri of past events.

Captured on a Box Brownie in 1954, this 1911-built steam tugboat displays her attractive lines while coming alongside the quay at Q Shed after towing the s.s. *Bayano* into port. Owned by C. J. King & Sons, *Bristolian*, 179 tons, served the Royal Edward and Avonmouth Docks well for fifty-six years and, in 1967, was offered to the City Council as a working museum attraction for just its scrap metal value. But the Floating Harbour's wharves were still bustling with commercial activity and the offer was turned down.   Now a recreation area, the City Docks are tragically short of port-related working vessels.

Three mates from the PBA engineering workshops on location maintenance work, November 1955. These little red and white electric trucks were a familiar sight around Avonmouth Docks during the 1950s and 1960s.

A gang of contented Bristol dockers prepare to discharge a shipload of aluminium at the Royal Edward Dock in January, 1973.

Running repairs ... Dennis Godwin tries to stitch up his pal, Ray Colston after the strain of unloading tea chests at T Shed caused Ray's jacket to go all to pot one frosty morning in November, 1973.

Tom Davies received a miniature forklift truck from fellow dockers, Fred Buck and Jack Canning, upon retirement in September, 1980. Tom was among the first to leave under the voluntary severance scheme which reduced the labour force dramatically in the 1980s.

The distinctive lines of the steam hopper *Frome*, 521 tons, can be seen in this silhouette picture from 1954 which shows her steaming past Portbury on her return to the City Docks after depositing a mud cargo in the Bristol Channel.   Built at Renfrew in 1900, the *Frome* and her sister ship *Avon* were well known to Bristolians for over half a century until replaced in 1957 by motor mud hoppers of the same names.

Brown mud in the sunset.   Yes, 1500 tons of it aboard the hopper *Kingroad*, heading out of Avonmouth Dock in autumn 1967 to deposit this unwanted cargo in the open sea.   The *Kingroad*, acquired by the Port dredging department in 1953, was sold in 1983, after modern pipe dredgers were introduced, and now works in the London river.

18 January, 1969. Mrs Thatcher, then Shadow Minister of Transport, visited and told General Manager, George Edney: 'if you have great faith in the West Dock, are confident of its viability and are prepared to find the risk capital, then it is up to you.'   Nine years later the dock opened for business.

The controversial M.P. Enoch Powell was shown around Avonmouth Docks on 4 July, 1969 by Avonmouth Docks Chairman Cllr Ted Wright and general manager George Edney.

General manager Stanley Turner explains the advantages of operating the new deep-water dock to Bristol West M.P., William Waldegrave, Shadow Minister Sir Keith Joseph and Cllr Sir Robert Wall during a visit to Royal Portbury Dock in June, 1978.

John Major toured the extensive acreage and modern facilities at the Royal Portbury Dock on 11 September, 1996.   The Prime Minister commented: 'I am very impressed with the Port's continuing success and have enjoyed my visit to Bristol.'

No longer required by C. J. King & Sons to tow shipping to and from the City Docks, the *Sea Gem* was beached at Portishead Dock in 1967 and broken up for scrap metal.   Her sister tug, the *Sea Prince*, had a decade earlier been run down and sunk by the m.v. *Cato*.

The Bristol dockers' rowing team race past St Anne's Board Mills during a summer evening in 1970.   The rowing club, with its boathouse at Welsh Back, was a popular attraction in the docks.   The board mills, once so vital to the economy of the City Docks because of its voracious appetite for woodpulp, were closed by the end of the 1970s and later demolished.

Welcome home – and what a mighty reception the 127-year old s.s. *Great Britain* received as she approached the entrance of the Royal Edward Dock on 23 June, 1970 after a 7600-mile journey from the Falkland Islands. Thousands of proud Bristolians cheered her here, and along her journey up the Avon to the very dock where she had first been launched all those years before.

The 1073-ton Trinity House vessel, *Patricia*, whose full-time role was to service lights and buoys around the United Kingdom, rounds Horseshoe Bend after her annual visit to the city in May, 1970. A pretty little ship, she has since been replaced by a modern, but less attractive, namesake.

Despite the smiles, few were enthusiastic about leaving the PBA's Queen Square offices early in 1972, to be relocated to the industrial suburb of Avonmouth.

This stately stairway at the port's Queen Square headquarters – used by the Docks Commitee, important visitors and senior staff – led to the board room and other high places.

This custom-built Port Office was officially opened on 2 December, 1971. It brought together staff from Queen Square and the Avonmouth Docks office.

This battered footbridge and level crossing at Avonmouth Dock railway station were part of the Gloucester Road scene from 1907. The crossing was the cause of countless delays to traffic and port people every time a train went through and sealed off the road. The gates were manually operated from a small cabin alongside the track until lift barriers were introduced in June, 1973. The big white gates were hauled away and, six months later, the sixty-six-year old bridge was demolished.

Signing off ... when the Avon Bridge finally opened to traffic, the Pill ferry – the more attractive way to transverse the banks of the Avon – was doomed. Bob Brown, owner of this ancient means of transport, cheerfully accepted the inevitable as he was photographed aboard his motor boat *Margaret* on 1 November, 1974. A few hours later, with ferryman Albert Sharp at the helm, the *Margaret* eased herself clear of the Shirehampton slipway and made her final voyage to Pill.

After many delays the final span of the M5/Avon Bridge was hoisted into position as the evening light faded in March, 1974. This motorway link was extremely beneficial to the Port of Bristol, linking the entire dock system and opening up new commuter possibilities.

(top left) H.R.H. Prince Philip with Lord Mayor Cllr Hubert Williams and project chairman Richard Gould-Adams at Wapping Dry Dock, 28 May, 1975.

(top right) H.R.H. Princess Margaret was welcomed by Port Director Gordon Scott Morris in May 1984, when a luncheon was hosted in her honour by the St Helena Shipping Company of which the Princess was patron.

(bottom left) H.R.H. The Princess Royal, president of the Missions to Seamen, visited the Mission centre at Avonmouth on 6 October, 1989.

(bottom right) Port directors Terence Mordaunt and David Ord were presented by Sir John Wills to H.M. The Queen when she visited the Royal Portbury Dock in June, 1995.

Sea of smiles – the PBA Football Club won the prestigious Berkeley Hospital Premier Cup after defeating Cam 4-1 at Sharpness on 1 May, 1976.   The PBA fielded four active football teams in the 1970s, and as many cricket teams.

Turned out nice again ... Bristol's new Lord Mayor, Cllr Jack Fisk and Bristol Docks Committee's new chairman, Cllr Wally Jenkins seem confident of happy times ahead as they address a Docks Committee meeting in June, 1976.

Twins – the 542-ton mudhoppers *Frome* and *Avon* were well known to many Bristolians as they worked their way around the reaches of the Floating Harbour alongside the bucket dredger *Samuel Plimsoll* for twenty years, maintaining deep-water berths and preventing the dock silting up.   Eventually, modern pipe dredgers sucked the mud from under them and the dredging duo became redundant.   They are pictured in 1977 in the equally redundant locks of Avonmouth Dock just before being sold off.   In 1992, they were spotted, still up to their gunwales in glorious mud, at Milford Haven.

Harry Brown, 634 tons, steams past Pill and under the Avon Bridge towards the open sea to dredge up another cargo of sand and gravel from the bed of the Bristol Channel during February, 1977.   Built in 1962, *Harry Brown* was a familiar sight to Bristolians until sold in 1990.   In the foreground is a section of the United Molasses plant at Avonmouth Dock.   Five years later, this company moved across the river to Portbury and occupied a new 53,000-ton capacity storage and distribution centre.

The Lord and Lady Mayoress, Cllr and Mrs Marmaduke Alderson, were presented with a PBA clock and heraldic shield by Port Director, Nasim Ahmad and Chairman, Dr Doug Naysmith, after an official tour of the docks in July, 1987. The Lord Mayor, anxious to help promote the port during his year of office, was invited to participate in the ceremony celebrating the half-millionth car to come ashore at the Royal Portbury Dock.

The last social event to be held at the Port of Bristol's Police Club took place on 30 June, 1989, when 30 policemen assembled to bid farewell to the popular Sergeant Roy Harney. Large retirement gatherings were a frequent, almost weekly, event back in the days when many hundreds were on the Port payroll.

Bristol bows out ...HMS *Bristol*, the seventh ship to bear the name, is pictured leaving port on 10 June, 1991 on her last visit to the City of Bristol before a final voyage to the breakers. The 6000-ton destroyer – the most powerful missile ship in the Royal Navy – had been commissioned eighteen years earlier, on 31 March, 1973 during a forty-five-minute ceremony at L Shed, Avonmouth Dock – the first time a warship had been commissioned in Bristol.

Local colour ... tugs *John King* and *Mayflower*, together with fire boat *Pyronaut,* added much to the excitement of the International Festival of the Sea at the City Docks during 24-27 May, 1996. 700 ships and boats from around the world – along with side events, water displays and fireworks – created a wonderful carnival atmosphere for the 368,000 visitors over the four days.

There could be no better way to celebrate the 500th anniversary of John Cabot's epic 1497 voyage to the New World than to recreate it.   In May, 1997, a Bristol-built replica of his ship *Matthew*, pictured sailing past the modern Port of Bristol, will pay tribute to the great explorer by casting off from the Bristol quayside to cross the North Atlantic bound for Newfoundland.

Index

Acina 153
Akademik Sechenov 153
Akaroa 100
Alain L.D. 144
Alaric 28
Albright Explorer 65
Albright Pioneer 64-6
Angelic Grace 144
Angelic Protector 144
Antenor 97
Apollo 54-5
Ariguani 75
Arrow 26, 132, 135, 138
Arthur Albright 64
Athellaird 52
Athelmonarch 51
Atlantic Superior 147
Auckland Star 106
Avon 4, 7, 9, 12, 14, 17, 19, 25, 27, 32, 41, 49, 57, 63, 71, 103, 131, 150, 165, 167, 170, 172-3
Badminton 22
Balmoral Castle 119
Baltkon 14
Banglar Swapna 119
BD7 32
Beltimber 146
Benefactor 115
Birmingham City 50
Biscaya 32
Border Terrier 84
Bristol City 4, 51, 78-9, 83, 86, 91-2, 94
Bristolian 10, 52, 111, 120, 163
Bulk Enterprise 89
Cabot 9, 19, 27, 88, 100, 175
Calgaria 78
Captain Veniamis 150, 154
Cardiff Queen 13
Cato 16, 167
Cavina 76
Ceramic 93
Chailey 64
Charente 26, 28
Chennai Jayam 102

Chennai Ookkam 81
Churnuca 33
City of Auckland 106
City of Bristol 51, 59, 174
City of Chelmsford 74
City of Gloucester 109
City of Lichfield 117
City of Newcastle 99
Clan Chisholm 74
Clan MacGregor 123
Clan MacTaggart 75, 77
Clifton 50, 65, 72
Corinna 156
Coventry City 83, 92
Craftsman 120
Cyclops 97
Dagmar Bratt 13
Demeterton 95
Dido 11, 27
Dock Express 12, 148
Duhallow 157
Dunster (Temple Lane) 90
Echo 56, 93, 119
Emmy S 34
Endres Gane 74
Ernest Brown 55
Esbjorn Gorthon 16
Essex 5, 80-1, 151
Esther Del Mar 141
Falaba 116
Falgarth 82
Fana 51
Finnish Wasa 104
Flag Mersindi 158
Flecha 156
Fort Royal 137
Fraternia 24, 26
Free Enterprise II 109
Frisian Explorer 125
Frome 7, 9-10, 14, 165, 172
Furunes 127
Geestbay 123
Geestport 124
Gertrude Bratt 20
Gladstone Star 55
Gloria 33
Gloucester City 79

Gothic 83
Great Britain 2, 4, 10, 42, 49, 71, 110, 131, 154, 167
Grebbestrom 21
Gripsholm 110
Halifax City 91
Hardwicke Grange 48
Harry Brown 42, 173
Havpil 11
Hero 26-7
HMS Bristol 162, 174
HMS Fife 134
HMS Flying Fox 17, 41
HMS Hecate 42-3
HMS Hecla 45
HMS Sealion 28
Honmoku Maru 146
Hotwells 9, 12, 39-41, 44, 49, 57, 65
Hvalvik 115
Imke 29
Indian Trust 118
Inga 33
Ionic 105
Irene 21-2
Irisbank 88
John King 13, 28, 32, 110, 175
Joseph P. Grace 112
Judith-A (fomerly Conroy) 17
Juno 49, 55
K.C. Rogeraes 76
Kelvin 8, 23
Kenn 32
Kingroad 165
Kiwi Arrow 132, 135, 138
Kulpawn River 58
Kungsholm 110, 136
La Ensenada 141
La Sierra 143
Lady Betty 22, 24
Laurentian Forest 103
Leader 55
Leander 16
Logos 46, 151
Lossiebank 79
Loussio 155
Mansart 121

Margaret 170
Marinus Smits 35
Martaban 77
Master Nicos 88
Mathew 50, 60
Mathraki 145
Mayflower 175
Mercury 174
Mergui 104
Merrimac 58, 76, 115
Michurinsk 55
Milo 17, 90, 93
Montreal City 50, 91-2, 94
Nakwa River 110
Nancy Raymond 93
Neva 32
New York City 86
Nonsuch 94
Offin River 105
Oosterburgh 35
Ortega 119
Ortelius 139
Osaka Bay 142
Otaio 113
Patricia 168
Pengarth 48, 144
Peter Leigh 110
Peterston 44
Pluto 12, 21, 23
Point Gilbert 144
Point James 148
Polgarth 105
Port Brisbane 84
Port Chalmers 85, 120
Pyronaut 175
Pytchley 160
Queensland Star 57
Regent Panther 74
Renwick 30
Research 50
Resolute 91, 162
Rhodesia 31
Rimba Balau 127
Rockhampton Star 57, 107
Royal Yacht Britannia 131, 134, 162
Salacia 74
Salisbury (BP11) 81
Sally Organ 93

Samuel Plimsoll 44, 172
Scol Spirit 68
Sea Alert 27, 107
Sea Bristolian 111
Sea Challenge 52, 120
Sea Gem 167
Sea Merrimac 58, 115
Sea Queen 96
Sea Volunteer 58, 107, 111
Seatrain Rotterdam 136
Seijin 148
Severn 32, 57, 72, 78, 82, 162
Somerset 9, 63, 113
Southern Cross 155
St Helena 128, 171
St Vincent 65
Stadf Wolfsburg 109
Stanford 17, 19-20
Steep Holm 23
Stena Paper 31
Stentor 115
Strinda 138
Sussex 103
Talisker 8
Texaco Kentucky 112
Texaco New Mexico 107
TFL Express 130
The Shoots 57
Thelm Leigh 162
Toba 159
Toronto City 92
Tourcoing 139
Troilus 77
Tucurina 112
Vard 36
Volunteer 13-14, 58, 107, 111
Wani Swan 158
Westgarth 74
Westmorland 55, 102, 119
Woodlark 22
World Sea 96
Zaanborg 21
Zenit 19